Gandhi
on
Personal
Leadership

**39
Powerful
Lessons**

D1460649

**From the life & times of
India's visionary leader**

Anand Kumarasamy

JAICO PUBLISHING HOUSE

Ahmedabad Bangalore Bhopal Bhubaneswar Chennai
Delhi Hyderabad Kolkata Lucknow Mumbai

Published by Jaico Publishing House
A-2 Jash Chambers, 7-A Sir Phirozshah Mehta Road
Fort, Mumbai - 400 001
jaicopub@jaicobooks.com
www.jaicobooks.com

© Anand Kumarasamy

GANDHI ON PERSONAL LEADERSHIP
ISBN 81-7992-571-4

First Jaico Impression: 2006
Tenth Jaico Impression: 2016

Printed by
Repro India Limited
Plot No. 50/2, T.T.C. MIDC Industrial Area
Mahape, Navi Mumbai - 400 710

This book is dedicated to my Parents & my Sister.

This is what you shall do: Love the earth and sun and the animals, despise riches... devote your income and labor to others, hate tyrants, argue not concerning God, have patience and indulgence towards people.... re-examine all you have been told at school or church or in any book, dismiss what insults your very soul, and your very flesh shall become a great poem.

WALT WHITMAN

Contents

Acknowledgments

First of all, I would like to thank my parents and my sister for their love, patience and forbearance. Dear Mom and Dad: for giving me the freedom and the opportunity to follow my dreams, I am forever indebted to you.

I want to thank my dear friends in Mumbai, India. I still vividly remember that warm sunny day in Khadakvasna, India, when we were sitting in Vineet's beautiful house overlooking the lake and I announced to all of you that I was writing a book. Your enthusiasm, encouragement and belief in me were positively overwhelming, to say the least. Thanks to all of you guys, from the depths of my heart.

I wish to express my deepest gratitude to Peeran Mukadam. Thanks for believing in me. You are a great friend, and I am a better person for knowing you.

Special thanks to Carolina Rivera. Your support, encouragement and guidance have been invaluable assets in helping me complete this book.

Thanks to Andrew Shedden, Asim Ali, and Corin Raymond for reviewing earlier portions of this manuscript, and for your honest feedback and suggestions.

Last but not least, I would like to thank Lesa Wright, who helped proofread this book and went the extra mile to make helpful changes to and suggestions for the manuscript.

1

Introduction

You my friend, a citizen of this great and mighty city of Athens, you devote yourself to acquiring the greatest amount of money, honour and reputation, and yet you care so little about wisdom, truth and the greatest improvement of the soul, which you never regard or heed at all?

- Plato, Apologia

An increasing number of people are growing tired of the frantic pace and pressures of modern life. In spite of all the unprecedented material comforts we enjoy as a society, a strong sense of incompleteness pervades the lives of many people in our culture. The oft-heard complaint is that something crucial seems to be missing. The old, traditional assumption that material wealth and scientific progress can, by themselves, lead to happiness and true fulfilment is being questioned by a growing number of individuals. People today, more than ever before, are yearning for a purpose beyond mere profits — a meaning beyond money.

This disillusionment with modern life is fuelling a powerful, contemporary spiritual quest for greater substance, fulfilment and authenticity, and it is for this reason that books on the meaning of life and spirituality routinely hit the bestseller lists. Some examples of such books in recent years are *What do I do with my life?* by Po Bronson, *How to know God* by Deepak Chopra and *The Purpose-Driven Life* by Rick Warren. Interest in yoga, tai chi and meditation has gone up tremendously. Moreover, as people become increasingly aware of the perilous state of the planet, environmental degradation, the loss of a sense of community, religious intolerance and hatred and the increasing gap between the rich and poor, there is a growing realisation that the old ways of thinking and perceiving must change. Indeed, as Einstein stated, *a problem cannot be solved from the same level of thinking we were when we first created it.*

This book attempts to provide some principles, ideas and alternatives that can help us in our personal quest for greater substance and also help address some of the pressing social and ecological challenges of our times. It studies the life of one extraordinary individual, Mahatma Gandhi, and emerges with 39 powerful lessons of personal growth and transformation. These lessons, gleaned from Gandhi's life, offer us invaluable advice on leading an enlightened life — a more meaningful, self-aware, socially responsible and saner life.

"Why Gandhi?" you might ask. Besides being the chief architect in the Indian struggle for freedom, Gandhi evolved the unique way of "Satyagraha" (soul force or truth force), a highly effective method of civil disobedience and non-violent resistance that was intended to be an alternative to violence and designed to bring about positive social and political change. More importantly, Gandhi envisioned a world that would evolve towards peace and harmony — a world where different religions, cultures and peoples of the world would live together with mutual respect and tolerance, rather than in suspicion and animosity. In a century marked by two world wars, the holocaust and the atomic bomb — when the world was torn apart by hate and intolerance — Gandhi emerged as a powerful antithesis to man's cruelty and small-mindedness. He became the voice of sanity, and a beacon of hope for peace-minded and tolerant individuals everywhere.

Although Gandhi was by no means perfect (he had his share of faults and flaws), he made significant and seminal contributions that span across such disciplines as economics, spirituality, conflict resolution, politics and more. His name has become synonymous with non-violence, social justice and civil disobedience. Most notably, Gandhi and his method became inspirations for Martin Luther King, Jr. and Nelson Mandela in their respective freedom movements.

Gandhi's contributions, his achievements and his life were extraordinary by any measure. Most importantly, however, Gandhi's life offers us vital lessons on living a meaningful, purpose-driven, and morally awake life. He lived his life seeking truth and wisdom and, like Plato, he cared for "the greatest improvement of the soul." In studying his life, a very clear set of principles, ideas and convictions emerge. I have attempted to encapsulate and distil them into lessons that can be integrated into our lives. These are enduring and timeless lessons that transcend time period, place, person, culture or economy. As such, they are very timely and relevant to the concerns and issues of our time — perhaps more so than at any other time.

This book has four core objectives.

- One is to *inform* the reader about the life of Gandhi. This book traces the life-journey of one man from being a timid, young child to the visionary leader who bequeathed to the world a novel method of fighting oppression, thus becoming an inspiration to millions in India and abroad.

- Secondly, his story and the lessons therein are intended to *inspire* us to stretch beyond ourselves, and to get in touch with the power that lies hidden within us. Gandhi's life offers compelling evidence that we can become the conscious shapers of our own destinies, rather than being merely shaped by circumstances.

Thirdly, this book is an attempt to *remind* us of what 'the better angels of our nature' are capable of. Every day, we see and hear news of human immorality such as corporate corruption, exploitation, religious intolerance, violence and impending ecological disasters precipitated by society's greed and apathy. In such a scenario, people like Gandhi are powerful reminders of the greater capacities and farther reaches of the human spirit.

- Fourthly, it is a psychological and philosophical study that aspires to be a *guide* for our own journey of self-discovery, maturity and learning. It is a roadmap for all those who are in pursuit of a more meaningful existence. The process of personal transformation seldom happens "by accident"; it is the product of conscious choice. Therefore, I have outlined many vital lessons from Gandhi's life that are both timeless and universal, and these essential lessons have formed the bedrock of some of the most productive lives ever lived.

This book will start with a short biography of Gandhi, which highlights some of his formative experiences and a few of his most important achievements. It then clearly outlines the lessons of personal growth and transformation that we can learn from his life. In order to explain and illustrate these lessons, I have drawn from a diverse range of fields such as psychology, management, leadership, philosophy and spirituality. I have tried to present the lessons in a simple, succinct, easy-to-read and interesting manner. Finally, while I have not specifically described any practical techniques or exercises, I have listed books and resources at the end of this book — some of which contain very good exercises, tools and techniques that one can use to fashion positive changes in one's life.

One last thing before we begin: given the complexity of such a life as Gandhi's and the relative brevity of this text, I am profoundly aware of the limitations of this book. Many of Gandhi's core ideas and principles such as "Swaraj," "Sarvodaya" and "Satyagraha" are complex and nuanced, and are not greatly touched upon here. His own definitions underwent a constant expansion as he made these ideas more complete and comprehensive through constant experimentation and practical application over the years. I have only skimmed the surface of these ideas, to give you a very basic introduction to them. If you would like to delve deeper into those ideas, there are a number of books and articles that explain and analyze these themes in greater detail. You will find many of these resources on the Internet and at your local library.

Let us now begin....

2

Mohandas Karamchand Gandhi; A Brief Biography

Hate does not cease by hate. By love alone it ceases.
This is eternal law.

- Buddha

Mohandas Karamchand Gandhi was born on October 2, 1869 in Porbandar, a small seaside town on the shores of the Arabian Sea in India. His family, for many generations, served in provincial governments as prime or home ministers. Gandhi, the youngest of four children, was by his own confessions a painfully shy and fearful child. He writes in his autobiography,

> *I used to be very shy and avoided all company. My books and my lessons were my sole companions. To be at school at the stroke of the hour and to run back home as soon as the school closed — that was my daily habit. I literally ran back, because I could not bear to talk to anybody. I was even afraid lest anyone should poke fun at me[1]*

He even admits to a childhood fear of darkness, and an inability to sleep without a light on in the room. He confesses,

> *Moreover, I was a coward. I used to be haunted by the fear of thieves, ghosts and serpents. I did not dare to stir out of doors at night.[2]*

Gandhi's childhood was not unlike those of many others. He went through a brief rebellious phase where, at the convincing of a friend, he took to eating meat in secret (a practice strictly forbidden by his community), tried smoking and even visited a brothel (although he writes of being so paralysed with fear that a lady showered abuse upon him and had him thrown out). But soon his better sense prevailed, and Gandhi gave up these novelties and experiments.

Gandhi was married at the "preposterously early" age of 13, under the Hindu tradition of child marriage — a custom that Gandhi grew up to vehemently oppose. His young wife, Kasturba, was also 13 and had a mind of her own; their early relationship was marred by discord, thanks in large part to Gandhi's unfounded suspicions, jealousies and possessiveness (as admitted in his autobiography). Regarding the marriage itself, Gandhi, at that tender age, saw it naively as nothing more than having a "strange new girl to play with." The young boy was enamoured by the marriage feasts, the colourful clothes, and the processions. Gandhi soon became besotted with his new wife:

> *I must say I was passionately fond of her. Even at school I used to think of her, and the thought of nightfall and our subsequent meeting was ever haunting me. Separation was unbearable. I used to keep her awake until late in the night with my idle talk.[3]*

While his wife was in the later stages of pregnancy, Gandhi spent most of his time after school tending to his sick father. He loved nursing, and would sit by his father's bedside massaging his feet, until he slept. Gandhi writes of finding it difficult to control his sexual desires, noting that

*Every night whilst my hands were busy massaging
my father's legs, my mind was hovering about the
bedroom, — and that too at a time when religion,
medical science and common sense alike forbade
sexual intercourse* [4]

One night, overcome with desire, he left his father's side
to be with his wife. No sooner did he leave his father's
bedside and go to his conjugal room, there was a knock
on his door. Gandhi was informed that his father had died.
Gandhi was heartbroken that he had not been by his father's
side at that crucial moment — and to add to his woes, his
and Kasturba's child died within three days of being born.
Gandhi blamed himself and writes that he never got over
this "double shame." His inability to control his passions,
when it most mattered, weighed heavily on him for the rest
of his life. In his words, it was *a blot I have never been able
to efface or forget.*[5]

Meanwhile, Gandhi's mediocre grades meant his future
was not looking too promising. He was at a crossroads of
sorts when a relative suggested that Gandhi study law in
England. Gandhi grabbed the opportunity with both hands
(so to speak). After much controversy and debate within
the community, Gandhi was allowed to go, but only after
he had vowed to his mother that he would keep away from
meat, alcohol and women. Gandhi made this promise, and
looked forward to this new life of adventure and "a long
and healthy separation" from his wife. In 1888, a raw,
young Gandhi — all of 18 years — set sail for England.

Gandhi's shyness was a major impediment in his travels. On
his way to England, Gandhi stayed away from conversations
with fellow passengers on the ship. Self-conscious and
unable to speak English, he even had his meals in his
cabin, which were mostly sweets and fruits that his mother

had packed for him. His early days in England were full of loneliness, and he writes of being terribly homesick. It was daunting for the young man to learn a new language, and to adjust to new food, new customs and a new culture. From the small town of Porbandar to the hustle and bustle of London (which was, at the time, the largest city in the world) was overwhelming and highly challenging. But slowly things took a turn for the better.

Since he had vowed to his mother that he would not touch meat, he sought out vegetarian restaurants in London, and found one after much searching. He also joined the vegetarian society and was a part of its executive committee. Nonetheless, Gandhi remained quiet at meetings, feeling awkward and tongue-tied when asked to offer his opinions to the group. He would write out speeches and somebody else would read them aloud. All the same, he began to form some friendships and acquaintances.

It was during his time in London that he also began his exploration into matters of religion. He had been an atheist in his younger days, since most of what he saw as religion were oppressive customs, rules and laws that only curtailed his freedom. Now, he began to take an interest in religion and spirituality, discussing it with his small but growing group of friends and acquaintances. He had traversed the "Sahara of atheism," and was now hungry for something of substance. Around this time, he was introduced to the Bhagavad-Gita, a sacred text within the Hindu tradition. It was "love at first sight" for Gandhi, who wrote that *the verses in the second chapter made a deep impression on my mind, and they still ring in my ears. The book struck me as one of priceless worth.*[6]

The Gita is an epic poem set amidst a battlefield where Arjuna, the warrior, finds himself in the unenviable position of having to fight against his own brothers and close relatives. The sight of his brothers arrayed against him and the very thought of having to kill them drives Arjuna to deep anguish, and he sinks to his knees in utter despair. His charioteer and friend, Krishna — who is the representation of the Universal Self — comes to his rescue. What follows in the Gita is profound metaphysical and practical advice: as Krishna expounds on the meaning of life, the struggle of the human soul on its upward ascent, and the prescription to knowing one's true self (i.e., yoga). Gandhi himself was to say that the Gita is an allegory and it used the battlefield as a metaphor representing "the duel that perpetually went on in the hearts of mankind."

The Gita became his spiritual staff and support until the very end of his life. It was his rock-solid companion, pulling him out of his dark days and inspiring him in the despairing moments of his life. Years later, he would write that

...when doubts haunt me, when disappointments stare me in the face, and I see not one ray of light, on the horizon, I turn to the Bhagavad-Gita, and find a verse to comfort me; and I immediately begin to smile in the midst of overwhelming sorrow. My life has been full of external tragedies and if they have not left any visible or invisible effect on me, I owe it to the teaching of the Bhagavad-Gita.[7]

Back in England, some Christian friends gave him the New Testament. The Sermon on the Mount profoundly affected him, and he also read the biography of the prophet Mohammed; they all whetted his appetite for religion. Strikingly, Gandhi's spiritual foundations at this point were being laid, and he was already beginning to glimpse the underlying unity that existed among all these diverse and great religions. It was this ability to see beyond the superficial — to see a deeper unity amongst human beings and religions — that would become his hallmark, his signature inclusive style. His natural tendency was towards *uniting* rather than *fragmenting.*

He was also slowly moving out of his "comfort zone" (that space in which we all find ourselves in the *status quo*). He developed a small but diverse group of friends and acquaintances. He started a vegetarian society, visited France, and most importantly, continued to introspect on issues of right and wrong, values and ethics. Because of his interests in morality and his desire to apply them to his own life, he was constantly noticing instances, both small and big, where he found himself not being truthful, and he would make efforts to set them right. Within the vegetarian society, he stood up to support a member who was unjustly asked to leave the society. Although he failed, this was the first instance wherein Gandhi took a thoughtful, principled stand in a public sphere, risking unpopularity in the process.

Of course, Gandhi's main reason for coming to England was to study law. Although Gandhi was not an exceptional student, he applied himself diligently and learned Latin and French along with his law degree. He passed his bar examinations and his time in England came to an end, but he still deeply doubted his ability to stand up in a court of law and argue a case convincingly. Gandhi's early life was quite mediocre and uneventful and, at the age of 21, there were still no overt signs of greatness.

Having completed his studies, Gandhi returned to India. Upon his arrival, he was given the heartbreaking news that his mother had died while he was away. His brother had withheld the news to spare him of the shock while in a foreign land. Gandhi was deeply pained, but he buried his grief and attempted to set up his law practice in Bombay. But Gandhi was not very successful because he could not get over his shyness and fear of speaking in public. He attempted to eke out some semblance of a career, doing legal paperwork and drafts. Obviously, the Gandhi that we've all come to know had not yet surfaced.

After two years of unsuccessfully attempting to set up a law practice in India, Gandhi received a chance to help out with a legal case in South Africa. In 1893, Gandhi — who was now 24 years old — once again set sail for a distant land. This time it was South Africa — another British colony — and he thought he would be back soon. Little did he know of the momentous changes his life was about to undergo.

In South Africa

Gandhi's early experiences in South Africa made it clear to him that it was not a very hospitable nation for a person of colour. While his Indian employers and colleagues treated him warmly, he soon had his first brush with overt racism, when he was thrown out of a first-class railway compartment car, though he held a first-class ticket. Indians were simply not allowed to travel in first class, which was reserved exclusively for whites. This event would prove to be a watershed moment in his life.

Gandhi soon found out that the experience such as he had had on the train was not new to Indians. All people of colour were treated as second-class citizens — and sometimes worse. Indians were called condescending names such as "coolies" and, even in official books, as "semi-barbarous Asiatics." Indians could not remain out at night without a permit, nor could they walk on the footpath at any time of day. Most Indians had become used to such differential treatment and

Gandhi was told by many to "pocket this insult" and ignore it. But such events and experiences only served to increase his sense of moral indignation. He writes that

> *I saw that South Africa was no country for a self-respecting Indian, and my mind became more and more occupied with the question as to how this state of thing(s) might be improved.*[8]

Meanwhile professionally, Gandhi began to mature and blossom. He diligently applied himself and learned the basics of the case he was assigned to. He developed his knowledge, both theoretical and practical, of the law. Most significantly, his confidence in his abilities and capacities had increased dramatically. In his first case since coming to South Africa, he noticed that although his client's case was strong, a lengthy court case would be financially ruinous to both parties. Moreover, the defendant and plaintiff were relatives, and their relationship was becoming increasingly strained. Gandhi successfully convinced both of them to negotiate a compromise out of court. He writes triumphantly that

> *I had learnt the true practice of law. I had learnt to find out the better side of human nature and to enter men's hearts. I realised that the true function of a lawyer was to unite parties driven asunder.*[9]

Gandhi steadily began to develop a good reputation and won the trust of his community. The cornerstone of his law practice was attempting to bring about private compromises between the parties involved. He writes, *I lost nothing thereby — not even money, certainly not my soul.*[10] He was fast becoming a well-respected lawyer who was known for his principles and ideals. With his contract in South Africa coming to an end, Gandhi was persuaded by his friends and clients to stay back to help them protect their rights and civil liberties. A collective body called the Indian Congress of Natal was formed. Their first assignment was to oppose a bill that was soon to be passed, which would take away even the existing civil liberties of the Indian community. It was at this point that Gandhi was pulled into the social and political field. He began to hold meetings, draft petitions, and publish and edit newspapers highlighting the plight of Indians in South Africa. All this experience, as it would be proven in India, was invaluable for Gandhi.

Meanwhile, ideals and principles such as simplicity, service to the poor, non-violence and sacrificing smaller impulses to achieve greater goals was beginning to take root within Gandhi's mindset. He began to simplify his lifestyle and changed his diet as he matured in spiritual and moral awareness. He volunteered to be a nurse at a hospital so that he could satisfy his thirst for service. He accepted no. money for his community work, and even liquidated any expensive gifts he received and invested it in a trust fund for the benefit of the Indian community. He was also beginning to learn that self-control and discipline were necessary, if one were not to respond to one wrong with another — an act which he felt solved nothing and only served to increase the spiral of violence. As he was to say, *an eye for an eye only ends up making the whole world blind.*

Gandhi read widely, drawing inspiration from such diverse sources as the Bhagavad Gita, Sermon on the Mount, John Ruskin and Leo Tolstoy. In order to put into practice the ideas and principles from these books, Gandhi started the Phoenix farm, an experimental community made up of a diverse group of Britons, white South Africans, and Indians. It was a microcosm of the ideal world, at least as imagined by Gandhi. The farm was founded and managed on the bases of service, equality of all and the dignity of labour. As a result of these experiments, his inward transformation began to accelerate, and manifest itself in his outer work.

Meanwhile, the political and social repression of Indians in South Africa was reaching new heights with each passing day. The government had proposed a bill that, if passed, would mean that any Indian could be deported from South Africa under the smallest pretence. It would give to the police draconian powers that would allow them to enter Indian homes at will and even search women. It was restrictive, humiliating and, if passed, could mean the beginning of the end for Indians in South Africa. Gandhi convened a meeting attended by 3,000 people to discuss their future options.

The Indians seethed with anger as Gandhi started to speak. He stated that it was *better to die than to submit to such a law*. Even as Gandhi was speaking, all his past work — the inner momentum that had built up — erupted from within. Spontaneously, and almost without thinking, Gandhi stated that they would defy the law, but not retaliate with violence. They would adhere to the highest possible standards of conduct, but not yield in their demand for equality. Gandhi gave an inspired speech, and the force and conviction with which he spoke won over his audience. Every man and woman pledged and took a sacred vow to offer non-violent resistance to the very end. *Thus came into being*, Gandhi later declared, *the moral equivalent of war*.

Gandhi began to call this method "satyagraha," meaning *firmness in truth*. Rather than brute force, the weapon would be *soul force or truth force*. Abhorring violence, one would disobey the "unjust laws," even if it meant risk to one's life and limb. Such a method, in his opinion, would not only stem the tide of violence, but the self-suffering would also appeal to the heart and conscience of the one who inflicts the suffering.

Gandhi's methods were based on the fundamental assumption that man's nature is innately good. As Nelson Mandela has pointed out, *Man's goodness is a flame that can be hidden but never extinguished.* Gandhi had a deeply abiding trust in that goodness, and his methods were suited to speak to that goodness within humans. But in order to do so, one had to be courageous, highly self-disciplined and, above all, truthful and non-violent in thought, word and deed. "Satyagraha" appeals to the conscience within the opponent — to the "God within" — and it attempts to awaken in the other a moral sensitivity. Gandhi never tired of saying that non-violent struggle or Satyagraha Was not a possibility for the weak or the cowardly; it was only for the wise, the courageous and the disciplined.

On many occasions, Gandhi led long marches, broke what he considered were unjust laws and courted arrest; he refused to cooperate with the upholders of the law. As a result, Gandhi found himself in prison on more than one occasion and it was while in prison that he read Thoreau's essay on civil disobedience. Henry David Thoreau (1817-1863) was an American writer, philosopher and naturalist from Concord, Massachusetts. Thoreau himself had spent a night in jail because he refused to pay a poll tax; he did so as an act of disobedience against the American government's position on the Mexican War and slavery. He put forward his ideas and convictions in his essay entitled civil disobedience, and it is this work, which Gandhi read. Although they had lived in different eras and in different countries, both men shared the deeply-held conviction that they should disobey a law that their conscience (the higher law) told them was unjust.

Convinced that he was headed in the right direction, Gandhi intensified his spiritual, political and social activities. Around this time, Gandhi also wrote for and helped edit a newspaper called Indian Opinion. He emerged as a strong, trustworthy and morally upright leader for the Indian cause in South Africa. Even Indians back home were beginning to take notice. Gandhi continued the struggle in South Africa over the next decade, putting considerable pressure on the South African government to reverse its oppressive laws. The only thing Gandhi refused to do was resort to violence or untruth.

It was at around this time that another major aspect of the Gandhian method would reveal itself. During the Indian civil disobedience campaign, the South African railways, completely unconnected with the Indians, went on strike. The government, already struggling because of the Indian strike, had its resources spread thinly, and it was at its wit's end. Gandhi, rather than continue his campaign and bring the government to its knees, immediately called off his campaign under the principle that it would be unfair to take advantage of an opponent's weakness or attempt to humiliate them. This move was welcomed by the British, and congratulations poured in on Gandhi. More importantly, it opened the door for negotiations, and Gandhi was invited by the government for discussions. The deadlock was thus broken, and a settlement was reached.

In the year 1914, the South African government made important concessions to the Indian community. Gandhi felt that his work was done and was contemplating heading back home to India. His friends in India — with whom he was in regular contact — were persuading him that his real work awaited him there. It was not just that India needed him, but he felt he needed India too, for his spiritual growth and awakening. His inner prompting to "see God face to face" was growing louder. He had left India thinking that he would be back in a year; instead, he had stayed in South Africa for 21 years. Now his homeland was beckoning him.

India was a land where more than 90 percent of her people lived in villages. The entire Indian system of landlords and administrators, together with the British overseers, were ruthlessly exploiting the poor and underprivileged. For decades, poverty-stricken farmers and other small labourers did backbreaking work, but had nothing to show for it — and then there was the even greater evil of "untouchability which kept the poorest of the poor chained to their miserable conditions. (The subject of untouchability will be discussed in greater depth later in this book.)

Nehru, the first prime minister of an independent India and a protégé of Gandhi who had been brought up in the midst of wealth and opulence, writes movingly about the India that confronted him on his visits to the rural areas. Everywhere he went, the poor would greet him, deeply grateful that someone had come to listen to their genuine grievances. He writes,

> *Looking at them and their misery and overflowing gratitude, I was filled with shame and sorrow, shame at my own easy going and comfortable life and our petty politics of the city which ignored this vast multitude of semi-naked sons and daughters of India, sorrow at the degradation and the overwhelming poverty of India.[11]*

The poor seemed to be long forgotten. For centuries, nothing but poverty, death and disease was their lot, and their cries went unheeded. Now, however, Gandhi was heading back to India with his tried-and-tested methods. Indeed, hope was on the way.

Back in India

In 1915, Gandhi arrived back home to India. He then slowly began to get involved in social and political activities. He once again began to organise civil resistance campaigns, mostly at the local level, to address injustices that affected farmers and labourers such as the Champaran struggle in Bihar, and the dispute between management and workers at a textile mill in Ahmedabad. Gandhi was successful in helping bring about a successful resolution in both these instances. Due to the successes of these and many such campaigns, his fame began to spread and Gandhi soon found himself leading the Indian independence movement.

Meanwhile, British brutality was steadily increasing. In 1919, hundreds of unarmed civilians, including women and children were brutally shot dead at a religious rally in Amritsar in Northern India. Gandhi called for a nationwide civil-disobedience campaign. He urged Indians to boycott British products, stop paying taxes, and to forsake British titles and honors. This placed the British under considerable pressure. But the campaign was marred by a singular incident of violence when a group of policemen were killed. Gandhi deeply disturbed by this violence immediately suspended the movement. He was, nevertheless arrested on charges of sedition, and sentenced to six years imprisonment. He was released after two years.

Upon his release, Gandhi withdrew partially from national politics and concentrated more on social activism. He established an Ashram (a place for social work and spiritual practice) and also started a newspaper called *Young India*. He was working to socially uplift the poor and marginalised by helping open small village industries, cooperatives and so forth that encouraged self-sufficiency. Over the following

32

years, he toiled incessantly to preserve Hindu-Muslim relations, and in 1924 he observed, a 21-day fast when Hindu-Muslim riots broke out In Northern India. Through out his life, he went on many such public fasts, and in 1932 he undertook his famous "epic fast unto death", for the eradication of untouchability.

Meanwhile, the clamour for Indian independence was steadily growing within the country. In 1930, the Indian National Congress, the leading political force in the Indian independence movement, declared that Indians would now be satisfied with nothing short of complete independence. Gandhi launched a nation wide civil disobedience campaign beginning with his now famous salt march to protest the imposition of tax on salt. He along with thousands of people marched 240 miles to the coastal town of Dandi to collect their own salt in defiance of this "unjust law". This march is considered to be one of the most remarkable events in the history of modern India. (I have written about this event in greater detail later in this book).

The Satyagraha campaign would continue for well over a decade. In the year 1946, 16 years after Dandi, Britain — economically depleted by the war—announced that they would be leaving India. However, India would soon be partitioned and Pakistan a separate nation for Muslims was to be created. Gandhi who had worked unceasingly for Hindu-Muslim unity was vehemently opposed to this plan. But it was adopted and approved by the Indian National Congress, the Muslim League (a political party representing Muslims) and the British.

In the year 1947, as the partition of India was becoming a reality, tensions between Hindus and Muslims grew. Large parts of the country descended into chaos as groups within both the Hindu and Muslim community resorted to arson, loot, rape and murder. It is now widely agreed upon by historians that Gandhi's actions during this period, in many respects were nothing short of magnificent. He fasted in Calcutta, where the violence was at its worst and within days the riots ended. What was called the great Calcutta killing was now the great "Calcutta miracle". He then walked from village to village in the riot-torn district of Noakhali, nursing and consoling the victims who had lost their loved ones and urging people to give up violence. In the words of Lord Mountbatten, India's last viceroy, Gandhi became a "one-man boundary force" between Hindus and Muslims. (I have written about the Calcutta fast in greater detail in another chapter).

On January 30,1948, Gandhi, escorted by his two nieces — on his way to a prayer meeting — was shot three times in the chest. Gandhi fell to ground, as he uttered the words, "He Ram" (One of the words for God in Hinduism). His assassin was a fanatic belonging to a Hindu extremist group that had been angry at what they perceived to be Gandhi's bias towards Muslims.

At the time of his death, his personal possessions were valued at less than two dollars; he held no office or title, and was lovingly called "Bapu" (father) by millions and venerated with the title "Mahatma" (great soul). As a shocked nation attempted to come to grips with this tragic loss, heartfelt messages of condolences and grief came pouring in from all over the world. Among so many other accolades, he earned from George C. Marshall the deserving title, *spokesman for the conscience of all mankind.*

Albert Einstein wrote,

> *He [Gandhi] has demonstrated that a powerful human following can be assembled not only through*

the cunning game of the usual political manoeuvres and trickeries but through the cogent example of a morally superior conduct of life. ...in our time of utter moral decadence he was the only statesman to stand for a higher human relationship on the political sphere. [12]

Martin Luther King Jr. wrote many years later, *Man has thought twice in our century: once with Einstein, then with Gandhi.* He added,

If humanity is to progress, Gandhi is inescapable. He lived, thought and acted, inspired by the vision of humanity evolving toward a world of peace and harmony. We may ignore him at our own risk.

LIFE LESSONS

3

A Strong Sense of Purpose

Life is no brief candle to me. It is a sort of splendid torch, which I have got a hold of for the moment, and I want to make it. burn as brightly as possible before handing it on to future generations.

- George Bernard Shaw (1856–1950)

When we look at the lives of certain people – people such as Mahatma Gandhi, Mother Teresa, Albert Einstein and Martin Luther King, Jr. – we notice a certain similarity that they all shared. They all submitted or dedicated themselves to a greater purpose, a noble cause, a worthy endeavour that transcended the boundaries of their narrow self-interests. It was this overarching sense of purpose that gave meaning to their lives and brought about a deep and abiding sense of fulfillment. In his critically acclaimed book, *The Farther Reaches of Human Nature*, Abraham Maslow studied the characteristics of self-actualizers, and found that virtually all self-actualizing people such as Mahatma Gandhi, Eleanor Roosevelt, and Albert Einstein were committed to "a cause outside their own skin."[1] They were all passionately devoted to a greater calling. They had a sense of mission that was bigger and beyond them.

Mahatma Gandhi's mission, for example, was to win freedom for India from British rule through non-violence, and also to create a more just and exploitation-free social order. Mother Teresa's calling, similarly, was to serve the diseased and dying, and through them serve God. Likewise,

Martin Luther King Jr.'s dream was to win civil rights for African-Americans and create a unified America. Gandhi, Mother Teresa, and Dr. King are three names from a long list of eminent personalities who dedicated their lives to a purpose that went beyond the boundaries of "I," "me" and "mine." Indeed, a truly great mission or purpose begins with and includes the *self* but it ultimately transcends it. As the celebrated Irish playwright George Bernard Shaw wrote,

> *This is the true joy of life, the being used for a purpose recognized by yourself as a mighty one.... the being a force of nature instead of a feverish, a selfish little clod of ailments and grievances complaining that the world will not devote itself to making you happy.*[2]

Gandhi's life is a prime example of how a strong sense of calling can become one's rationale for living. He was deeply committed to achieving India's freedom by non-violent means. He envisioned an India where people would live in peace and harmony; this became the dominant theme of his life, his fundamental priority. This compelling cause became the end towards which his whole life was directed. Great people like Gandhi *sign up, take a stand, volunteer, commit, dedicate and devote* themselves to a worthy endeavour. Their lives become instruments for a larger purpose — vehicles for achieving something that truly matters.

The seed for Mahatma Gandhi's mission was first sown when he was 24 years old, in South Africa. He was on his way from Durban to Pretoria, South Africa, for legal business. Being new to the country, he was unaware that coloured passengers could not travel in the "whites only" first-class section. On that journey, Gandhi was ordered by the conductor to move to the third-class section, even though he had a ticket for the first class. Gandhi declined to move and was thrown out of the train at a small station in the middle of the night. He sat alone on the platform on a long, cold winter's night, shocked and humiliated by this fierce display of racism and institutionalized prejudice. Many years later, Gandhi recalled this event as one of the defining moments of his life. It was this event that opened his eyes to the injustice and discrimination that Indians were subjected to in South Africa. It helped him clarify his mission and calling in life.

A powerful sense of mission gives our lives a clear sense of direction. It takes all our energies – which are normally diffused – and gives them a laser-like focus. That energy becomes a rich source of motivation and inspiration. Rain or shine, it becomes the reason that we get out of bed every morning to boldly face the challenges of the day.

A strong sense of purpose can accomplish three things for us. Firstly, it can be a rich source of happiness. It can lead to a healthy sense of self-esteem, and a sense of fulfillment that is derived from doing something that truly matters to us. Secondly, it can make life worth living, enabling us to overcome the inevitable adversities that we face in life. Finally, it helps us transcend the work-joy dichotomy. When we are doing something that we truly, deeply care about, work becomes the same thing as play. Let us explore these three points in finer detail.

1. A strong sense of mission is a rich source of happiness, self-esteem and self-fulfillment.

Some of the things that we most yearn for in our lives are happiness, peace of mind and a sense of fulfillment. We spend our days trying our best to find the ways and means through which we can be happy. The pursuit of happiness, it can be said, is the number one preoccupation of all human beings, and yet it has proven largely elusive to the vast majority of us. This is because the search for happiness is paradoxical: the more we pursue happiness directly, the less likely we are to find it. But when we dedicate our life to a cause that is. greater than us, we see that happiness ensues automatically, by itself.[3] History shows us that people who live a life of significance and worth do not chase directly after happiness; rather, they develop a powerful sense of mission in their lives. In other words, happiness is the *residual result, the unintended side effect* of leading a purposeful life – a life that is committed to serving an end that is bigger and beyond one's self.

Devoting one's life to a worthy cause is the most effective antidote against the sense of meaninglessness that pervades so many lives in our day and age. People who are wholeheartedly pursuing something that truly matters to them will, inevitably, enjoy better health, vitality and energy. They are less likely to fall ill, and even when they do, they recover and bounce back much more quickly than others. Leading a purposeful life contributes to a healthy sense of self-esteem – a sense of significance and self-worth.

When such a sense of purpose is lacking, egocentric preoccupations with "I," "me" and "mine" play havoc with our happiness. One begins to become obsessed with body image and social status. Such trivial concerns as smoother skin or our place on the social ladder begin to take centre stage. The unbridled thirst for money; power, privilege and fame often become our ultimate concerns. Life becomes an unhealthy self-absorption that takes away from our happiness, rather than contributing to it.

The urge to accumulate large amounts of material wealth, power and fame are all essentially concerns of the ego. In the absence of an overarching mission in our lives, our ego becomes the master and dictates the terms of our lives. In self-actualizing people, we see the exact opposite: in these greats, the ego is put to work in the service of something that is bigger and beyond it. The ego may be a bad master, but it is a good servant. Ultimately, life comes down to making a simple choice: we can either submit our ego to a course greater than us, or let the unchecked greed of the ego dictate the scope and direction of our lives. Therein lies the difference, between a happy, fulfilled life, and a life spent in perpetual dissatisfaction.

Rather than seeking happiness directly, it is far more effective for us to seek meaning in our lives and to live according to our inner standards and values. Happiness is the natural by-product, the organic result of attempting to live our lives in accordance with our deeply-held values, guided by a powerful sense of mission. When we seek to live the right way, happiness and fulfillment often come by uninvited, of their own accord. Gandhi derived his sense of self-worth – his sense of happiness, fulfillment and meaning – by dedicating his life to a greater purpose that was in sync with his core values and beliefs.

2. A strong sense of purpose makes life worth living.

The first of the four noble truths that Buddha taught is "life is difficult." This will hardly come as a surprise to most of us; pain and suffering are no strangers to anyone born into this material world. We are all well aware that we do not always get what we want in life, and that failures and setbacks are inevitable. As human beings, we are all vulnerable to loss, illness and unhappiness. But when we have something to live for, we are able to overcome the inevitable setbacks, pain and suffering of life. A strong sense of purpose makes our life worth living. Take the example of Viktor Frankl, a distinguished psychologist from Vienna, Austria.

Frankl was among the few men and women who survived and made it out of the brutal and horrific conditions of the Nazi concentration camp during World War II. In his book, *Man's Search for Meaning,* he writes of the nightmarish conditions in the prison camps where starvation, torture, and death became the norm. Being a psychologist, Frankl noticed something very crucial: while many of the physically stronger prisoners perished, the ones who survived were those with a powerful sense of purpose. Those who made it out of these camps alive were the ones who felt that they still had some unfinished work in life, something to look forward to. It was this compelling sense that they had something left to do that intensified their will to live.[4]

Mothers with children are less likely to commit suicide than women without children. This is a telling statistic. The knowledge that another life depends on them – that they cannot let their children down – keeps these mothers going. Even though they may suffer from psychological and emotional problems and are often tempted to give up, they hang on and seek help because they know that they cannot desert their children.

Throughout his life, Gandhi faced many setbacks, both personal and professional. Like all of us, he suffered from bouts of doubt, and there were times when he was tempted to give up the struggle. But he knew he had to soldier on – not for himself, but for the sake of the poor and hungry millions in India who were suffering under the weight of the unjust British rule, the caste system and an exploitative economic structure. In Gandhi, the poor and downtrodden saw hope, and he knew that. He seemed to be the long-awaited answer to their prayers. The simple notion that so many people were depending on him, were pinning their hopes on him, kept him going. He knew that he could not leave the job unfinished. It was this strong sense of calling and belief that became one of his greatest sources of stability. It helped him hold steady and stay on course amidst the roughest seas, and ride out the fiercest storms. Throughout the epic Indian freedom struggle, great setbacks appeared, and many seemingly insurmountable hurdles turned up. But it was this greater purpose that carried him through adversity and the moments of doubt.

3. A sense of mission enables us to transcend the work-joy dichotomy.

In our society today, a substantial number of people state that they are dissatisfied with their jobs. This is a tragic statistic, considering that we spend much of our adult life at work. When we work on jobs that are deeply dissatisfying, it inevitably spills over into other areas of our lives and affects our families and other relationships. When we are doing jobs that do *not* truly, deeply matter to us, we become "clock watchers" at work, wondering when it will be time to leave. Work becomes a chore, and we simply go through the motions. Our hands may be at work, but our head and heart are elsewhere. We start living for the weekend. Rather than experiencing joy at work, we experience frustration, resentment and anxiety. As French philosopher and novelist Albert Camus wrote, "When work is soulless, life stifles and dies."

Ultimately, job dissatisfaction can affect our physical health. Studies suggest that the best predictor of heart disease among men is not high cholesterol or blood pressure, but rather job dissatisfaction.[5] Also, more fatal heart attacks occur on Monday mornings at around 9:00 a.m. (at the start of the work week) than at any other time of the week. This phenomenon is known as the "Black Monday Syndrome."[6] This occurrence suggests that these people are so dissatisfied with their jobs that they dread going back to work after the weekend. While outwardly they may be able to feign interest, their body does not lie.

One of the main reasons why so many people find their jobs dull and boring is because they have made the search for money and profits their primary motivation in life. Our culture has implicitly assumed that the ultimate purpose of life is material comfort. It equates money with happiness and fulfillment. Such a view is myopic, shallow and one-dimensional. We are creatures desperate for meaning; without meaning, we cannot grow, develop or mature towards health. Viktor Frankl founded an entire school of psychology called "logo therapy"; it is based on his observation that our search for meaning is the "primary motivation" in our life.[7] Money and profits alone cannot quench our deeper thirst for meaning. As Frankl notes, most of us in the western world have the means but not the meaning.[8] Thus, while money and recognition are important, it cannot be our primary motivating factor in life. Money and profits cannot gratify our urge for creative expression. They cannot quench our thirst for meaning and significance. They do not address our need to serve, to contribute, and to make a significant difference in the lives of others, or to leave behind a lasting legacy.

Great people like Gandhi do not choose their life's work based on conformity to societal dictates, fads and fashions. They are not fixated on the mere economic value of work. Rather than asking what job would pay well, or which job is held in high social esteem, they ask what they truly want to do, and would love to do. They look for a *meaning beyond money, a purpose beyond profits*. In so doing, their work becomes an avenue for expressing their creative abilities and talents, and they derive a deep sense of significance and joy from their work. To them, there is no difference between work and play. The work-joy dichotomy disappears.[9] Many of us assume that joy is found outside of the work situation, but never within it. But for self-actualizing people, joy is derived from the work itself. Gandhi was once asked why he never took a vacation; he answered, "I am always on vacation." Or, as Thomas Edison, the prolific inventor who had a record 1,093 patents in his name stated, "I never did a day's work in my life, it was all fun."

There has been a notion – an idea as ancient as man himself – that presupposes that each of us is born for a reason, and that we have a unique meaning to fulfill in this life. According to this belief, we all come into this world with certain unique talents, potentials, capacities, and inner resources, and with distinctive ways of expressing them. We have a unique and specific contribution to make in our allotted time on this planet. This truth, while it cannot be scientifically proven, can be seen and sensed in the lives of great men and women.

When we look at the lives of pioneers, visionaries and creators – people who have made highly creative and original contributions to society – we cannot help but think that they were born to do what they do. They bring to their life's work a level of passion and commitment that is unparalleled. Whether it is Gandhi marching with staff in hand for the cause of freedom, Mozart at work on his music, or Sigmund Freud laying out his psychological theories, one gets the distinct sense that it is exactly the work that they were born to do. The fit is so perfect that one cannot imagine them doing anything else. Another example in our own times is the actor Al Pacino: one cannot imagine him doing anything other than acting. There is a distinct sense that we get when we see him on the screen: acting was what he was born to do. While they may never claim arrogantly that they were born for this reason, nevertheless, the quality of their work speaks eloquently for them.

Ultimately, work must be an avenue for our self-expression. It must be a reflection of who we are. It must be aligned with our deeply-held values and beliefs. So long as we are not expressing ourselves and living up to our inner potential, we will feel incomplete – and no amount of wealth or power will amend that.

In summary, what we have learned so far is that, as human beings, we all seem to need a sense of purpose, some worthwhile goal that will give meaning to our lives and make our lives worth living. As Spanish Philosopher José Ortega y Gasset stated, "Human life by its nature has to be dedicated to something." History shows us that people who live lives of significance and worth, also strive for goals that are greater and larger than any narrow self-interest. Dedication to a mighty cause is the best recipe for happiness, and the most effective antidote against a sense of meaninglessness, anomie and nihilism. Committing to a worthy endeavour is the ideal way to overcome life's inherent challenges of pain, loss and suffering, when they do inevitably occur. Finally, when we look for a meaning beyond money – a purpose beyond profits – we often transcend the work-joy dichotomy. Work becomes play, and our lives become the better for it.

4

The Importance of Character

*Character, in the long run, is the decisive factor in
the life of an individual and of nations alike.*

- Theodore Roosevelt (1858–1919)

Gandhi focused on his character; he worked ceaselessly
on it. He concentrated his efforts on *who he was*, rather
than *what he possessed*. In direct contrast, many of us are
easily seduced into believing that our possessions matter
more than our character. We grow to be very concerned
about how the world sees us. We begin to value ourselves
according to our physical looks, the clothes we wear, the
cars we drive, the places we are seen in, the jobs that we
hold and sometimes, even the girlfriend or boyfriend we
have. These are all image-focused or possession-centred
concerns. This concern, when held exclusively, often leads
us to neglect a deeper, more fundamental part of ourselves:
our character.

Change, growth and maturity begin when the focus shifts
from *what we have to who we are*. Ultimately, character
and *not* image makes the person. It is our character — our
capacity to transform ourselves from within — that has the
greatest impact on the quality of our lives. As the German
philosopher Arthur Schopenhauer wrote,

*What a man is, contributes much more to his
happiness than what he has... What a man is in
himself, what accompanies him when he is alone,*

what no one can give him or take away, is obviously more essential to him than everything he has in the way of possessions, or even what he may be in the eyes of the world.

It is an exercise in futility to work on our behaviour and attitudes superficially, without looking deeply into the source from where these attitudes and behaviours flow. Focusing on image alone seldom works in the long run, because one's character flaws remain, fester and deeply impact the quality and effectiveness of our lives. Steven Covey, in his book *The Seven Habits of Highly Effective People*, calls these image-oriented activities the "social band-aids and aspirin" approach: they are short cuts and "quick fixes" that may address superficial symptoms, but they leave the underlying chronic problems virtually untouched.[1]

Great people like Gandhi choose to work on their character, rather than being concerned with portraying an image. They work from the *inside out*, because they understand that character is the foundation of success, happiness and meaning in one's life. They nurture and nourish good habits based on such principles as compassion, courage, service to others, humility, patience, simplicity, fairness, perseverance, and so forth. These principles are timeless, universal and self-evidently true (i.e., every great culture, past and present, and every great religious tradition, have recognised these principles and virtues as being vital and necessary to effective living). These traditions suggest that to truly transform ourselves, we must integrate these virtues into our daily lives.

This is not to say that reputation does not matter. Reputation does matter. It matters deeply. But a good reputation flows from having a good character. Character is the source, and reputation is the result. Many people mistakenly see it the other way around, and they attempt to build a good reputation by merely portraying .a good image to others, even as their characters remain deeply flawed. In the long run, this seldom works. As Abraham Lincoln stated, *Character is like a tree and a reputation like a shadow. The shadow is what we think of it; the tree is the real thing.*

A good reputation must be the result of a good character. To put it another way: character is the cause, and reputation is the effect. Ultimately, a good image or reputation will crumble if it is not backed up by good character. We may be able to "pose", "pretend" and project a good image for others. We may even get away with it from time to time. But a lack of character — the very lack of principled behaviour — will prove to be our undoing in the long run. This is because, ultimately, people can sense inauthenticity; they can sense when someone is "faking it," or when a person is trying to come across as someone he or she clearly is not. Thus, projecting an image of a good person without first invoking a corresponding change in character will come across as hypocritical and duplicitous.

For example, when Gandhi simplified his clothing by wearing a loincloth, it was *not* simply a strategy or tactic through which he could project an image of being poor — there was something deeper at work there. There is no doubt that Gandhi's simplified dress code added enormously to his popularity amongst the masses; however, if we were to study his life closely, we would notice that Gandhi simplified his dress not because of image concerns, but because of larger, deeper character-oriented concerns. His change in dress was not a single, isolated action; it was part of a larger process of his moral and spiritual growth.

Firstly, his strong sense of compassion would not allow him to live in material comfort while the rest of his country's citizenry lived in poverty and misery. Secondly, he saw himself as a trustee or a caretaker of the earth. He wished to live simply so that others are not denied their share. Thirdly, long before he started wearing a loincloth, Gandhi saw the virtue of simplicity as essential to spiritual growth, and thus he begun to integrate the principle of simplicity into his character. The process of simplifying his needs and wants had begun many years before, and the switch to a loincloth was a natural culmination of this process. In Gandhi's case, outward simplicity was the *organic result* of this inner transformation. Gandhi's change in clothing hence looked spontaneous and natural, and he seemed to be completely at home and comfortable with it. If Gandhi had attempted it merely as a matter of image, and merely to create an *impression* of simplicity, he would have sooner or later been found out. His actions would have come across as inauthentic, and the masses would have sensed this duplicity. But his effectiveness and impact as a leader were greatly enhanced because of the genuine change that had come from within. It flowed from his *character.*

Our culture is, in many ways, very image-obsessed. Everyday we are saturated and drowned in images and messages from the media suggesting that we must look a certain way in order to be happy, or own certain status symbols in order to show that we have "arrived" in life. Psychologists and cultural critics have long pointed out that the images in the media set impossible expectations on both women and men; they not only engender deep-seated feelings of inadequacy but also put pressure on us to conform to certain physical images or to popular stereotypes. Our huge expenditures on designer clothing, "power suits," anti-aging products, expensive cosmetics and status symbols are a product of this

insecurity. Our sense of self-respect can also become tied
to how we look and what we weigh; it has been pointed out,
for example, that one of the major causes of eating disorders
amongst women is the cultural emphasis on thinness as the
ideal for beauty.[2]

Furthermore, when we look at many of the "personal
success" books on the market today, we see that most of
them put great emphasis on projecting a smooth public
persona and developing a positive social image. Character
(or even the importance of character) often gets only
a passing mention. In these books, it seems that every
problem, great or small, has only one answer: *get yourself
an image makeover.* Image consultants advise people
on how to "look sharp" and "dress for success." We are
told to use the "power look" to overawe others and hence
influence their decisions in our favour. According to these
consultants, we must project an "air of confidence," create
an "aura of mystery," or make a "million- dollar first
impression" in order to achieve success in our professional
and social lives. These books tout image-focused activities
as the foundation for success, and they encourage the
reader to put on a performance for others. The core concern
is on appearances and presentation. *Looking good* is more
important than genuinely *being good.*

Overwhelmingly, the message is that appearances are
everything. It makes us neurotically obsessive and
preoccupied with physical and material concerns. We
start to define ourselves, almost exclusively, through our
looks, our material possessions, status symbols and social
position. To borrow the words of Deepak Chopra, rather
than being "self-referral" we become "object referral."[3]

In the final analysis, it is our character — not cosmetics
or clothing — that will determine the quality of our lives.

As Ralph Waldo Emerson wrote, *character is higher than intellect* — and as Heraclitus similarly stated some 2,000 years earlier, *a man's character is his destiny.* Character is central and image is peripheral. Character is primary and image is secondary. Character is foundational; image is residual. As Gandhi stated,

> *"All your scholarship, all your study of Shakespeare and Wordsworth would be vain if at the same time you do not build your character and attain mastery over your thoughts and your actions ".[4]*

It is not suggested here that it is wrong to work on our image, our personality or communication skills. Image-based activities and personality development are necessary. Nor is it wrong to want to enjoy some of the material pleasures of life. But we are indeed in trouble if these goals become the primary focus of our lives. If we begin to exclusively focus on these surface things and start to neglect the deeper parts of our character, we will pay the price in the long run.

Gandhi's primary emphasis, early in his life, moved from image-centred activities to character-oriented ones. As a 19-year-old law student in England, he initially tried to fit into the English lifestyle by dressing up as an "English gentleman." He spent money on expensive suits and ties, and spent a lot of time ensuring that his looks and clothing were appropriate with the fashions of the day. He began to take violin and piano lessons, not because he loved these instruments, but because it would make him appear sophisticated, and would thus enable him to fit into English culture. In short, even Gandhi himself initially focused on image.

But slowly, one could see a very distinct change in Gandhi. He began to shift his emphasis more and more to his character.

In South Africa, he began to simplify his life, attempting to bring discipline to his wants and desires. He developed his instinct to serve others by volunteering as a nurse during wartime. He built his trustworthiness by keeping promises, and by striving to be honest, reliable, and principled. He built up his courage to do the right thing, even if doing so made him unpopular. He tried at every turn to treat people with respect, civility and courtesy, and refrained from ridiculing, embarrassing or hurting others. He strove to be tolerant of differences, and he sought to shoulder rather than avoid responsibilities. These are all essentially character-based activities, and they contributed greatly to his sense of self- worth, happiness and effectiveness in the long run.

5

The Power of Our Everyday Choices and Actions

*Nothing great is created suddenly, any more than a
bunch of grapes or a fig. If you tell me that you desire
a fig, I answer you that there must be time. Let it first
blossom, then bear fruit, then ripen.*

- Epictetus (55 AD–135 AD)

Many of us hold the assumption — a taken-for-granted belief
— that "small" is synonymous with "inconsequential" or
"insignificant." We believe that small actions and choices
do not have much of a bearing on our lives. We think that it
is only the big things, the big actions and the big decisions
that really count. But when you look at the lives of all great
people, you will see that they built their character through
small decisions, small choices and small actions that they
performed every day. They transformed their lives by
working on their day-to-day behaviours slowly, steadily and
consistently. Their personal and spiritual transformation
did not occur in one giant felled swoop, or in one singular,
spectacular action. It happened more through a step-by-
step or day-by-day approach. They nurtured and nourished
their good habits and chipped away .at their bad habits, one
step at a time. It was their small day-to-day decisions, their
everyday choices and actions, that cumulatively added up
to make tremendous difference in the long run. Indeed, in
matters of personal growth and character- building, there is
no such thing as an overnight success.[1]

Growth always occurs through a sequential series of stages.
There is an organic process to growth and transformation

that cannot be circumvented. When we look at children growing up, we can see this process at work: the child first learns to crawl, then to stand and walk, and finally to run. As it grows, it masters each level and moves to the next. It goes through a sequential series of steps where each step is a preparation for the next; no step can be avoided or bypassed. The same is true in the natural world. We cannot sow today and expect to reap tomorrow. The soil must first be tilled, and then the seed must be planted. Next, it must be nurtured and nourished with enough water and sunlight, and only then will it grow, bear fruit and finally ripen and be ready to eat.

Gandhi intuitively understood this organic process, and used this natural law to his benefit. Gandhi grew in small ways, in his day-to-day affairs. He did not wake up one day and find himself to be the "Mahatma" (great soul). Gandhi did not start out as "the Gandhi" that the world came to know so well. In fact, there was nothing much in his early life that showed signs of greatness. But from his mid-twenties onwards he consciously, deliberately and consistently attempted to change himself, reform himself, and grow in some small way everyday. Day by day, hour by hour, he risked failure, explored, experimented and learned from mistakes. In seemingly small and large situations alike, he took up rather than avoided responsibility. Understanding that "a journey of a thousand miles begins with the first step," he seized each day and made it count.

People have always marvelled at the seemingly effortless way in which Gandhi could accomplish the most complex tasks. He exhibited a level of self-mastery and discipline that was astounding. It would, however, be wrong to claim that these things came easily to him. Many people saw him exhibiting his self-mastery, but did not see the years of practice and disciplined training that went into making his successes possible. Very few saw, up-close and personally, his trials, tribulations, fears, doubts and anxieties, or his inner efforts to overcome them. They saw the victory, but not the struggle. They saw Gandhi reaping the rewards but they did not see him tilling the soil, sowing the seeds or nurturing the plant. Only through years of patience, practice and perseverance — by working day in and day out on his habits — was the "effortless performance" made possible.

If one were to ask what the singular, defining moment in Gandhi's life was that made him the "Mahatma," we cannot answer that question; there was *no* single, defining moment. It was the aggregation of his daily choices, small changes, little actions and many defining moments that cumulatively added up over a period of time to determine the quality of his life and its impact. All his great actions had their genesis in smaller ones. No singular event or action can be credited as being the definitive or decisive reason he had such a profound impact on the world.

This is a common factor in the lives of all great people: by exercising their freedoms and choices in small ways, their ability to influence and impact their lives and their environment grows. Each of their small and seemingly insignificant decisions and actions, taken every day, adds up cumulatively to have a profound impact in the long run. By making these small decisions — small changes in their everyday affairs — they build a momentum that makes it easier for them to choose and act with conviction and courage when the large dilemmas and decisions arise. As Phillip Brooks writes, *character may be manifested in the great moments, but it is made in the small ones.*

By understanding this principle, we can move forward, with confidence, in the direction of our dreams. Often when our "ideal goal" looms too far from us, we become easily discouraged, disheartened, and pessimistic. However, when we choose to grow in small ways, and when we break down any great task into small steps, performing it becomes progressively easy. As John Shaw Billings (1838-1913) wrote,

> *There's nothing really difficult if you only begin —*
> *some people contemplate a task until it looms so big,*
> *it seems impossible, but I just begin and it gets done*
> *somehow:*

We can begin by choosing to grow in small ways, in our day-to-day affairs; from there we build up slowly but steadily. Each day brings the opportunity for decisions and actions that will hold value for us. Large actions will flow from the little ones; hence, rather than disregarding the little things and the minor incidents, we can use them to guide our own growth and maturity.

6

Intrinsic Sense of Satisfaction

The reward of a thing well done is to have done it.

- Ralph Waldo Emerson (1803–1882)

One quality that separates greatness from mediocrity is that great people have an interest in their endeavours that is intrinsic (i.e., born from within). They choose their activities and tasks, and have experiences simply because they are genuinely interested. Their primary pay-off comes from the activity itself, rather than any external pay-offs such as rewards and incentives. They derive an internal, mental-emotional-spiritual "income" from the experience itself — an income that makes any outside reward quite peripheral and insignificant.

Research suggests that excellence in any endeavour may be possible only when we are able to derive an intrinsic sense of satisfaction from the activity itself. In one study, art students were interviewed, while they were still in art school, about the reasons behind why they chose painting as a career choice. Some said that they loved to paint and derived great joy from painting; others said that it was a good way to become famous or make money. Many years later — when these students were tracked down again, to see how far they had progressed — it was found that the ones who were still painting after so many years were those who had derived joy from the very act of painting. This joy had enabled them to continue to paint throughout their life. In contrast, those who had joined art school primarily for fame or to make money had drifted away from painting after graduation.[1]

When we intrinsically care about the activity itself and the primary pleasure comes from being immersed and engaged in the experience itself, then excellence is possible in the long run. The more we love the activity for itself, the more we will return to it and practice it. People such as Gandhi see action as its own reward: they derive an innate joy — an intrinsic satisfaction, as it were — from the process itself. They do things not because they *have to,* but because they *want to.* They have the ability to enjoy the journey without becoming too obsessed with the destination. In their lives, there is as much emphasis on the path as on goal. In fact, the path *becomes* the goal. In Gandhi's words, *Satisfaction lies in the effort, not in the attainment. Full effort is full victory.*[2]

When we become engaged in an activity for its own sake, we open up to the possibility of getting into the state of "flow." In this state, one becomes absorbed in the activity itself, losing a sense of time. It is a state of peak performance, known among athletes and sportspersons as being "in the zone." Sportspersons describe that in such moments, they become so absorbed-with the task at hand that they feel as if time stands still and the spectators disappear. In this state, things happen almost effortlessly. The state of "flow" leaves one with a tremendous sense of fulfilment. Creative artists also often speak of this state when they are engaged in the creative act of painting, sculpting, writing poetry, acting, and so forth. The painter speaks of "becoming one" with the very process of painting, and actors speak of "losing themselves" in the process of playing a character. This state of "flow" is the prerequisite for the mastery of a craft, because it becomes the motivation, and it spurs one on to not only stay with the task, but to test one's limits. Psychologist Mihaly Csikszentmihalyi has been studying this state for more than two decades, and has brought together his findings in his best-selling book, *Flow: The Psychology of Optimal Experience*. He writes that this "flow state" is a highly enjoyable, productive and deeply fulfilling experience.[3]

Gandhi derived tremendous pleasure from the activities that he engaged in. Whether it was writing and editing his newspapers, books and magazines, spinning the charka (a spinning wheel used for spinning cotton), engaging in manual labour or walking long distances, he immensely enjoyed what he was doing. Whatever he did, he was wholly present to the task at hand. For Gandhi, the primary motivation was the task itself; there was no outer compulsion — only intrinsic motivation. Gandhi's life exemplifies the principle of picking and choosing our interests based predominantly on their intrinsic pay-offs, rather than on their external payoffs such as monetary rewards and other incentives.

Channelizing Anger

Anyone can become angry — that is easy. But to be angry with the right person, to the right degree, at the right time, for the right purpose, and in the right way — this is not easy.

- Aristotle (384 BC–322 BC)

Anger afflicts us all, and most of us have had trouble controlling it at some time. We have spoken words and taken actions in anger and in the heat of the moment that we have regretted later. Yet we also know intuitively that sometimes anger can be appropriate and even necessary. But as the above passage from Aristotle's *The Nicomachean Ethics* makes amply clear, the most difficult task is to control and channel that anger in appropriate, constructive ways.

Sometimes anger seems to be appropriate. For instance, many people in today's world are very angry at unscrupulous organisations and individuals who pillage and plunder the environment and bring harm to other beings in the name of "progress." Still others are angry at human rights violations and other gross atrocities carried out against human beings in different parts of the world. We are angered by these instances because they violate our senses of justice, fairness and compassion. This anger is proof that we care — *deeply* care. It is born out of compassion and concern for one's fellow human beings, as well as the environment that one lives in. But the important question is: what do we do with all that anger and indignation?

Gandhi did get angry, but about the right things. Gandhi's anger and indignation was provoked when he came face-to-face with prejudice and injustice, but he reacted creatively to this anger. Rather than let his anger degenerate into a personal lust for revenge, his anger evoked from him the creative, nonviolent and highly effective method of "Satyagraha." Gandhi realised that to respond in anger to these indignities would only make matters worse, or would merely address the symptom and leave the underlying problem untouched. Hence, Gandhi's method of non-violent resistance was designed to strike at the roots of violence, hatred and bigotry.

Similarly, Henry David Thoreau (1817-1863) also responded creatively when his anger was provoked. Thoreau was an American writer, philosopher and naturalist who, as an act of disobedience against his government's position on the Mexican war and slavery, refused to pay a poll tax to the government. Thoreau was angry with his government for supporting slavery, and rather than pay the tax, he spent a night in prison. He actively channelled his anger into writing his landmark essay, *Civil Disobedience*. In it, he put forward his deeply-held idea and conviction that it is the personal responsibility of the individual to disobey his government when it engages in immoral and unethical acts. This essay had far-reaching social and political impact around the world; it influenced and inspired both Gandhi and Martin Luther King, Jr. in profound ways, and helped them shape their respective struggles against injustice.

Gandhi consistently attempted to move beyond anger — to rise above it, and to transcend it. He knew that anger more often than not clouds our judgment and disables us from seeing the situation clearly. If unchecked, it increases violence and is ultimately destructive to both the individual and the environment. Therefore, he endeavoured to find a constructive solution to anger, attempting in the process to rid himself of the hatred and violence that anger promotes. He learned to constructively channel the energy of anger in positive ways. Gandhi likened anger to electricity which, if mishandled, can be very destructive — but, if controlled and harnessed intelligently, can be used for the good of all society.[1] As Gandhi wrote,

> *I have learned through bitter experience the one supreme lesson to conserve my anger, and as heat conserved is transmuted into energy, even so our anger controlled can be transmuted into a power which can move the world.*[2]

John Walsh, host of the long-running television show *America's Most Wanted*, and Candy Lightner, founder of Mothers Against Drunk Driving (MADD) are two great examples from more recent times of people who channelled their anger in positive ways.

In 1981, John Walsh's six-year-old son, Adam, was abducted and later found murdered. John Walsh struggled with the pain, grief and anger, but rather than allowing this anger and grief to destroy him, he channelled it into a constructive cause of helping other families find their missing children. Along with his wife, he founded the Adam Walsh Child Resource Center, a non-profit organisation dedicated to legislative reform. He has been instrumental in helping pass laws that make it easier for parents to find their missing children. Finally, through his television show *America's Most Wanted*, he has helped bring many of America's most notorious criminals to justice, by publicly spotlighting wanted fugitives and allowing the public to provide information and clues.

The story of Candy Lightner is no less inspirational. In 1980, her 13-year-old daughter, Can, was killed by a repeat-offender drunk driver (he had three previous drunk-driving offences). Deeply affected by this personal tragedy and propelled by her grief and anger, Candy Lightner founded Mothers Against Drunk Driving (MADD). Through her organisation, she lobbied to pass stronger anti-drunk-driving legislation. MADD has also been highly effective in raising the public's awareness of the dangers of drunk driving — and thanks in part to MADD's good efforts, the number of alcohol-related traffic fatalities has reduced significantly in America.

Both John Walsh and Candy Lightner became tireless advocates for their respective causes. The one similarity that they share with Gandhi is that they used their anger to bring about positive change. Rather than let their anger destroy them and others, they transmuted it. Theirs was not a blind revenge seeking or simply a lust of retribution. Such a reaction is destructive and ultimately harmful to both the individual and the environment. In all these cases, anger was transformed into a life-sustaining energy, and was ultimately healing to both the individual and society. They channelled their anger in courageous, creative and life-enhancing ways.

The Power of a Dream

Far better to dare mighty things, to win glorious
triumphs, even though checkered by failure, than to
take rank with those poor spirits who neither enjoy
much nor suffer much, because they live in the gray
twilight that knows not victory, nor defeat.

- Theodore Roosevelt (1858–1919)

In order to make something happen, there must first be a
dream — because, after all, not much happens without a
dream. When we look back into history, we see that behind
every great achievement was a dreamer who dreamed great
and mighty things. All great pioneers and visionaries were,
first and foremost, dreamers whose dreams contained a
touch of the impossible. Let us take the example of Gandhi,
who also dreamed an "impossible" dream. To dream of
freeing India from more than 100 years of British rule — a
powerful imperial power — was bold enough, but to dream
that that freedom could be achieved without a single shot
being fired was audacious. He planned to achieve what had
never been done in the history of the modern world — at
least not on the scale that he was proposing.

When dreamers announce to the world their visions,
they are often dismissed as "impractical," "naive,"
"Utopian" or "idealistic." Their ideas are met with
ridicule and disbelief. Society rejects their ideas,
because they lie outside the realm of what is considered
possible. "If it has not been done before, then it cannot
be done" is the unconscious motto of a vast majority

in society. But all pioneers, creators and explorers have thought otherwise. When Gandhi first announced his plan, initially, many Indians were puzzled. They found his notion preposterous, that freedom could be won through non-violent struggle. He was ridiculed as "that silly old fool," or "a saint who cannot lead us." Many of the press members, political experts, pundits and even close friends advised him that his methods would not work. But Gandhi went after his dreams. He dared mighty things.

What we call "development" or "progress" is the breaking of barriers on what is considered possible. What we take for granted in our day — things such as democracy, freedom, air travel, the Internet or just about any technological or social innovation — had at one time existed only as thoughts and ideas in someone's mind. Certain individuals dared to dream, and they had the courage to disbelieve the limits that were seen as insurmountable by others. For example, two centuries ago, people said that it was impossible that man could fly. They said things like, "if God had wanted man to fly, He would have given us wings." The Wright Brothers invented the first airplane, man did fly, and now air travel is taken for granted.

Most great decisions and ideas sound great only in hindsight. For example, Buddha left behind all the wealth, power, glory, pomp and splendour of a kingdom, and went to the forest to meditate, fast and contemplate on the meaning of life. Only in hindsight, when we know what the Buddha would later achieve, does his decision seem to be a stroke of genius. But at the time he left his castle, he may have been labelled as insane. We see similarly powerful examples in today's world of business: Bill Gates dropped out of one of the most prestigious universities, Harvard, to follow his dream. The decision paid off for him, but at the time it would have been considered a "reckless" decision.

Similarly, after World War II, two young Japanese men set out to create a world-class company in the field of electronics. The only problem was that Japan was in ruins after the war, and in the 1940s the label "Made in Japan" signified "cheap" or "extremely poor quality." This was a bold dream and some might say "very impractical." They began their business in a small rented room in a bombed-out department store in downtown Tokyo. This company is none other than "Sony," the multinational electronics powerhouse that seems to have made a habit of consistently launching innovative and breakthrough products.

Dreams (or day dreams) play a very important role in our lives. They provide us with a vision of what we want to achieve in life. Almost all of us have goals, or some idea about what we want in life; only a few of us have bold, daunting and audacious dreams and goals. Not only is it important for us to dream, but it is important to dream *great dreams.*

Why is it important to have mighty goals, to dream great dreams? When our dreams and visions have a touch of the impossible, it stretches us. It grabs and pulls us out of our comfort zone. It forces us to employ new and innovative ways to achieve our goals. It rescues us from the rut of mired familiar, dysfunctional ways of living. As Peter Senge states in his book *The Fifth Discipline,* "The loftiness of the target compels new ways of thinking and acting."[1] We are forced to "think outside the box."

Vision ignites passion; passion breeds courage

A vision is the pictorial representation of our dream. It is a picture of our "preferred future." It answers the question, *what do I want the future to look like?* When we paint a picture of the future for ourselves — a picture that is in sync with our deeply held values — it evokes a strong emotional response from us and it can spur us to reach out and be more daring.

Psychologists speak of something called the "resiliency factor" which speaks of some individuals being more mentally and emotionally resilient than others. Some have a higher stress threshold than others, and such people seem to withstand a greater amount of pressure without succumbing to it. But this resiliency factor is not fixed; our resiliency is malleable, and not predetermined. It is not written in stone. When we hold a vision that we deeply care about, it ignites our passion and we immediately tap into our inner reservoirs of strength and courage. The resiliency and the stress threshold level of that individual changes. Passion breeds courage. It unleashes the hero within us.

With Gandhi at the helm, India embarked on one of the most unique freedom struggles in the history of the modern world. With truth, compassion and non-violence as his only weapons, Gandhi took on the might of the British Empire. Gandhi painted a compelling picture of a free India — a united and truly self-reliant nation. This compelling vision slowly began to capture the attention and imagination of Indians. Although many people initially doubted the efficacy of his methods, they gradually changed their minds as they saw Gandhi lead by example. Because Gandhi spoke and acted authentically and from his deeply-held values, his vision resonated with fellow Indians. The vision of being free men and women struck a powerful chord in their hearts and minds. People began to commit to this cause in larger numbers with each passing day. At one point, it was no longer Gandhi's vision; it had become a shared vision. Gandhi also helped them understand that this was a struggle of historic importance: if Indians could prove that freedom could be won through the non-violent way, then it would be a message of vital significance for future generations. As Gandhi stated, *History is a record of perpetual wars, but we are now trying to make new history.*[2]

This shared vision lifted common men and women to greater levels of heroism and courage. These "ordinary" folk became so inspired that they bravely and willingly joined in the struggle for Indian sovereignty. They endured physical blows and assaults without retreating or retaliating. They joined in Gandhi's hunger strikes and marches. Many went to prison, lost their jobs and suffered material losses, but they soldiered on courageously because they could sense that history was being made, right before their very eyes. The feeling that they were participating in something sacred and profound elicited the very best from these men and women. Their courageous actions are not understandable unless one realises that a powerful vision can inspire heroic acts and extraordinary courage from even the most seemingly ordinary person. As the Yogic sage Patanjali said more than a thousand years ago,

> *When you are inspired by some great purpose, some extraordinary project... your mind transcends limitations... Dormant forces, faculties and talents come alive, and you discover yourself to be a greater person by far than you ever dreamed yourself to be.*

Gandhi himself was a very fearful and painfully shy child. His shyness continued well into his late twenties. He was so shy and fearful that at social gatherings, he could not make the simplest of speeches. At meetings, somebody else would have to read aloud what he had written. To top it all off, his first appearance as a lawyer in court was an unmitigated disaster: as Gandhi's turn came to speak, he found himself overwhelmed and tongue-tied. Although it was a routine case involving a small claim, Gandhi was petrified and unable to speak a single coherent sentence. As he stood silent and squirming in embarrassment, he could sense the whole courtroom laughing at him. He hurriedly got another lawyer to handle the case and fled the courtroom in disgrace. In his autobiography, he speaks of the innumerable occasions when he found himself in similar embarrassing situations, all due to his shyness.

And yet this person became the leader of millions. He became an extremely proficient speaker. He grew so self-confident that he was soon meeting and negotiating with very important and influential leaders, such as British viceroys and generals who were in the top echelons of power. What happened? How did this painfully shy and fearful person end up as one of the greatest revolutionaries of the 20th century? What triggered such a powerful transformation?

The answer is simple: when we care about something deeply, it unleashes within us immense courage; it inspires in us great daring, and we venture forth boldly; In such moments, the self- limiting thoughts in our head lose their power over us. The vision of a free India and a peaceful and harmonious world was so compelling to Gandhi that he was no longer a slave to his fictions and fears. Inspired by this dream, he rose to the occasion. He found his voice. His vision exerted a pull on him that compelled him to move out of his "comfort zone." It enabled him to overcome his shyness. He cared so deeply about issues of freedom and non-violence that he tapped into his inner reservoirs of courage, will power, and self-confidence.

Only when we have a great dream — a vision of what we want to accomplish — will we truly know the extent and the depth of our potential, our courage and creativity. Unfortunately, the reverse is also true: when we do not have an overarching vision, we cannot do much, even in the best of circumstances. Without a dream or vision, even the trivial becomes painful; molehills appear as mountains and mere winds seem like hurricanes.

9

The Importance of Risking Failure

A life spent making mistakes is not only more honourable, but more useful than a life spent doing nothing.

- George Bernard Shaw (1856–1950)

Gandhi did not see failure as catastrophic, but rather as a feedback mechanism. He understood that to learn, to create or innovate one had to risk making mistakes. Without experimenting, one cannot truly learn. Risk of failure is inherent to any creative endeavour, and many of us give up on our dreams because we fear failure. But the greatest lesson to be learned from creators and visionaries is that success and failure are inextricably linked, and when you block failures, you block learning. If you avoid experimenting for fear of making mistakes, you also block out innovation, creativity and discovery. As Einstein asked, *If we knew what it was we were doing, it would not be called research, would it?*

Visionaries, creators and innovators have a high tolerance for failure. They do not seem to connect it with unworthiness or powerlessness, as most people are wont to do. Their self-esteem does not plummet every time they make mistakes. On the contrary: they see their mistakes and failures as opportunities for learning. Research suggests that most successful business people have an average of two business failures before they actually make it. If you look at the lives of people who have built or created something of significance, chances are you will notice that they have gone through the process of making mistakes and had their share of "failures" in order to become successful. The more experiments we undertake, the more we will make mistakes. The flip side of this, however, is that the chance of a highly original creative breakthrough also increases. Hence, "failure" becomes an integral part of the visionary's arsenal. When Thomas Edison, the great American inventor, was working to create the first commercially-viable light bulb, he tried thousands and thousands of combinations and experiments without success. But he never gave up, in spite of all these failures. When someone mentioned to him that he had failed in spite of 10,000 attempts, he is said to have remarked, *I have not failed; I have found 10,000 ways it won't work.*

Looking back upon our childhood, we will note that any skill we picked up (such as learning to ride a bike, playing a sport, mastering a musical instrument, eating with chopsticks or writing), chances are that we never got it perfect the first time around. It took us many attempts, and with each attempt, we got a little closer to getting it right. As someone said it well, *if you are not failing, you are not learning.* The fundamental fact is that we learn through trial and error. As Aristotle stated, *Whatever we learn to do, we learn by actually doing it.*

If we want to create anything, or achieve anything of significance, we will have to try it many times before we get it right. And in that process, risk, uncertainty, failure and temporary dis-orientation are inherent and even necessary. Growth requires the ability to tolerate temporary disorientations, and learning by its very nature makes us feel vulnerable. Nonetheless, to succeed in any task, we must risk that vulnerability; we may have to risk appearing as a "klutz" initially, because any new activity feels awkward at first. But one goes through an awkwardness stage en route to becoming proficient. As Somerset Maugham stated, "Only mediocre people are always at their best."

Of course we can hold back, and although holding back may seem protective in the short run, we also give up valuable opportunities for growth, maturity and fulfilment in the longer term. As Helen Keller wrote, *avoiding danger is no safer in the long run than outright exposure. Life is either a daring adventure or nothing.*

Gandhi, like a lot of other extraordinary visionaries, interpreted setbacks and negative events as positive challenges. He saw them as "essentials" or necessities on the path to growth, maturity and self-actualisation. He saw setbacks as being both temporary and surmountable, and mistakes and failures as lessons rather than catastrophes. He experimented constantly in all areas of his life, and some of his most important experiments were with the method of civil disobedience and non-violent resistance. He began to experiment on a small scale in South Africa by organising marches, public meetings, courting arrests, etc. They worked well in certain cases, and they sometimes proved to be failures. The feedback that he received from these experiments enabled him to continuously improve and refine his method of Satyagraha; it proved invaluable in India, when he led the much larger, nation-wide civil-disobedience movement.

In their book *Built to Last*, business consultants Jim Collins and Jerry Porras describe the results of a very interesting study that they conducted. They wanted to study the successful habits of visionary companies — to research the reasons why great companies consistently out-performed their rivals. One of their findings was that visionary companies *encouraged their employees to take risks.* The message that the employees got was that personal initiative was important, and that it was okay to make mistakes. Using very clear-cut policies and practices that were consistent with their core ideologies, these companies created an environment that was conducive to innovation, creativity and risk-taking. Thus, the employees in these companies made mistakes but were also consistently coming up with new, innovative and breakthrough ideas and products, enabling these organisations to deliver superior results year after year. In fact, even many of the "mistakes" turned out to be very lucrative. Examples abound in these companies, where an employee set out to create a certain product and failed, but in that process discovered something else that then became the basis for another breakthrough product. Because of this spirit of experimentation and innovation in these organisations, the employees "stumbled upon" new discoveries through their "mistakes." The visionary companies made some of their best innovations not through detailed strategic planning but rather through experimentation, trial-and-error and by quickly seizing upon opportunities.[1]

In direct contrast, in companies that were competing with these visionary organisations, employees were afraid to make mistakes because they knew that they would be punished if they failed. This fear-filled environment suppressed or inhibited the creative and innovative spirit of its employees, and hence these organisations ranked a distant second to the visionary firms in terms of new product development and financial returns.

If we want to do something new — something that we have never done before — then that means we have to take a risk. Mistakes and failures are an integral part of the growth process. We can only learn by actually doing, from experience. As business consultant Marshall Thurber has stated, *anything worth doing well is worth doing badly in the beginning.*

10

The Value of Creative Tension

The test of a first-rate intelligence is the ability to hold two opposed ideas in the mind at the same time, and still retain the ability to function.

- F. Scott Fitzgerald (1896–1940)

People like Gandhi welcome tension into their minds; they entertain within themselves a sense of creative discontent. What is the source of this creative tension? We saw earlier that many of the greats, like Gandhi, have a compelling vision; they see in their mind's eye a picture of what they want to achieve, and their passion, courage and creativity is unleashed. But this is only one side of the coin. Vision also unleashes a great deal of ambiguity, uncertainty and tension. This is the other side of the coin. This tension is a result of the gap between our vision (how we want the future to be) and the current reality (the way things really are). Current reality often falls woefully short of our desired ideal, and there is often a yawning gap between *what is* and *what should be*. Vision tells us *what* could be; current reality tells us *what is,* things as they currently stand. This gap between the "now" and the "ideal" becomes a source of tension. This is a necessary tension, and all true creativity stems from this uncertainty.[1] A painter may envision the most exquisite image, but the current reality is a blank canvas in front of him. Ultimately, the tension gives rise to the painting itself.

All great creators understand that this creative tension is a prerequisite for any creative breakthrough. They welcome this tension because it enables them to create. Genuine peace of mind or happiness is not possible without this creative tension. It is an indispensable and integral part of growing, learning and maturing. Those who seek happiness while avoiding this tension want to get to the destination without taking the journey. This inner tension can be suppressed and denied, but ultimately for growth to occur, it cannot be avoided.

Let us take the example of Gandhi's vision. Gandhi's goal was to free India from British rule through non-violence, and also to create a united, peaceful, just, equitable and caring society. But the reality that confronted him at that time was daunting, to say the least: Britain was a powerful imperial power at that time, and the mighty British Empire stretched from Africa to Asia. India had been under British rule for more than 100 years, and to the British, India was the "jewel in the crown." Britain held India in a vise-like grip, for India was the largest of her colonies, and the domination of India was a symbol to the rest of the world of Britain's might and power. To make matters worse, there was hardly any sense of a collective, united identity among Indians; in fact, India was a deeply divided society, characterised by infighting and suspicion among the various ethnic, religious and caste groups. For example, no "upper caste" Indian, with the exception of a few, wanted to work together with an "untouchable." There were also language differences and differences in state loyalties and religious diversity, all of which divided the country further. Hindus and Muslims did not see eye to eye, and often violence broke out between the two. Finally, Indian women — who formed 50% of the country's population — were for the most part confined to the household. This was the disheartening reality that confronted Gandhi. There is no doubt that the gap between his vision and India's reality created an emotional tension within him.

In spite of all these difficulties, Gandhi stayed with his vision. It remained the dominant picture in his mind. The true test of creative genius is to hold onto both these pictures simultaneously — and Gandhi accomplished it. He never lost sight of his vision and goal, but neither did he deny the current reality. He acknowledged all the practical difficulties. Many of us, unable to handle the stress of these two contrary images, often give up on our vision or aim, and settle for far less then we had originally dreamed. But Gandhi stayed the course. In fact, he surmounted each one of his obstacles. He did create a sense of national identity that transcended state and provincial loyalties. He made a huge dent in the caste system, enabling people of all castes and creeds to come together and fight (in the non-violent sense). Under his leadership, women came out in large numbers and participated in the struggle for freedom. Finally, his doctrine of non-violence made a huge impact on his people, and proved to be a very effective means in fighting the British.

Gandhi had a lofty vision but he also faced the cold, hard facts without flinching. He did not ignore the harsh ground realities, nor did he allow his vision to waver. He kept both the vision and current reality in sight. He welcomed and embraced the creative tension that resulted.

11

The Power of Spiritual over Material

Nothing splendid has been achieved except by those who dared to believe that something inside them was superior to circumstance.

— Bruce Barton (1886–1967)

To create anything of significant worth, a human being must first become aware that he or she holds the capacity within to transcend outside circumstances and external limitations. The greatest lesson we can learn from pioneers, creators, innovators and visionaries is that by using our inner abilities (such as self-awareness, faith, hope, courage, conscience, free will, imagination, thoughts, ideas, ideals and attitude), we can transcend outer circumstances, situations and past conditioning.

While we may be powerfully conditioned and significantly influenced by our genes, our environment and our childhoods, we are not completely determined by them. To paraphrase Stephen Covey, we are the products of our choices and not products of our past.[1] When we believe that outer institutions and material realities are more powerful than we are, we become resigned to our fate. We are more likely to see ourselves as powerless victims, and we feel that one man or woman cannot make a difference against powerful institutions. Great people, however, do not let circumstances dictate to them. Creators, pioneers and visionaries transcend and triumph over outer determinants and conditions. People who have made a lasting and profound impact on humanity — who have changed the

83

course of history — have always believed that the human spirit is primary, and that outer circumstances are secondary.

The notion of consciousness being primary has been expressed in wise traditions and by many philosophers of the past. In the words of Emerson, *We become what we think all day long...thoughts rule the world.* Shakespeare stated that *there is nothing good or bad, but thinking makes it so.* Jesus said *as you think so you shall be.* The Buddha affirmed that *all we are is the result of what we have thought.* Last but not least, Einstein stated that *Imagination is greater than knowledge.* Gandhi is one in a long, prodigious list of luminaries who deeply felt that there is great power within human beings — in their consciousnesses. According to these greats, the outer world can be significantly changed by changing what is within us. Outer realities did not have "the last say," so to speak; inner realties did. These great people placed a greater value on the invisible and intangible world that lay within human beings than on things in the material world.

Most of us, especially in the modern era, place exclusive importance and emphasis on the external world. We attach great significance to outside events and external circumstances, and very little (if any) significance on inner forces such as faith, hope, courage, imagination and so forth. Too many of us assume that external situations, social circumstances and institutions are superior to the inner person, and to our internal world. We hold the belief that our circumstances in life solely determine our happiness. This has been a debilitating belief and a crippling assumption that leads to reactive living; it is a self-fulfilling prophecy that engenders and reinforces a sense of powerlessness.

Does man shape history or does history shape man? Throughout history, great philosophers, poets, prophets and scientists have debated this issue. But this debate on free will versus fate is no closer to being resolved today than in the past. We may never fully know to what degree human beings are free, or to what degree we are creatures of circumstance.

While this debate may never be fully resolved, what we believe defines what we expect from life. It is a self-fulfilling prophecy: if you believe that outer circumstances and events are more powerful, then we will feel extremely powerless and become mere passive victims. On the other hand, those who break free from the grip of fate are the ones who *believe* that they can. Hence William James, the pioneering psychologist, wrote, "My first act of free will shall be to believe in free will."

Gandhi's moral leadership accomplished what was thought to be impossible by many. Not many believed in this old man in a loincloth, who was spouting words about the power of love, compassion, truth and non-violence. How could this "half- naked fakir" — as Winston Churchill condescendingly called him — take on the might of the British Empire? His claim that freedom can be won without war or resorting to violence seemed laughable. Throughout his life, Gandhi had to deal with the press, political pundits and even some close friends Who advised him that his methods would not work. He was told that his plans were "impractical" or "naive." Time and again, people would say to him, "it is not possible."

While all these experts and colleagues saw a world of limitations and obstacles, Gandhi saw a world of possibilities. Gandhi placed a greater emphasis on the inner, spiritual reality while others placed a greater emphasis on the outer, material reality. These different worldviews created two completely different sets of expectations, and would therefore generate completely different realities. People saw themselves as merely passive victims, shaped by events and experiences, but Gandhi saw himself as the proactive shaper of events and circumstances, as a co-creator of reality.

Gandhi's life shows us that we can choose: we can consciously choose to become the proactive designers of our lives, rather than simply be designed by our experiences. We can change the scripts of our lives, rather than merely living out our borrowed and obsolete scripts of the past. We are conditioned by our personal history, but we can transcend it through our conscious choices. We don't have to be like rudderless boats that are at the mercy of the weather and waves. "I know of no more encouraging fact", wrote Thoreau, "than the unquestionable ability of man to elevate his life through conscious endeavor".

To further understand the power of man's internal capacities, we can travel back to the recent past. In the 1940s, Europe was under the power of the brutal Nazi regime led by Hitler. Jews and other visible minorities were being rounded up. Men, women and children were all huddled into cargo trains and sent to concentration camps, where they would be eliminated with chilling efficiency. Among these masses was Viktor Frankl, a well-respected psychiatrist in Vienna, Austria. Overnight, he lost everything he ever valued and suddenly found himself in the brutal, terrifying conditions of a concentration camp. Life became a bleak, everyday fight for survival.

Frankl lived to tell the tale of his trials and tribulations in his munificent and moving book, *Man's Search for Meaning*. He writes of the nightmarish conditions in the prison camps where starvation, torture and death were all around him. But there were a few men who, even in those horrific conditions, would give away their last piece of bread to a hungry comrade, or would walk through the camp offering comfort and solace to others. Frankl writes that these men were few, and were the exceptions rather than the rule. Nevertheless, they provided undeniable proof that while a man may be robbed of everything, one thing *cannot* be taken away from him: the ability "to choose one's attitude in any given set of circumstances." Appropriately, Frankl called this "the last of the human freedoms."[2] Each of these men *chose* what sort of person they would become.

In fact, Frankl's own survival is a classic example of the triumph of the human spirit. How did Frankl make it out of this ordeal alive? He faced the reality of his situation, but refused to give into hopelessness or nihilism. He *chose* his attitude and responses. He intensified his inner life by exercising his awareness and imagination. For example, he imagined with vivid detail that he had survived the prison camp and that he was in a classroom, giving a lecture on his experiences to students. At other times, while he was subjected to hard labour in the biting cold, perpetually starving and semi naked, he brought forth to his mind the image of his beloved wife and held conversations with her. He could almost feel her palpable presence with him. He remembered the life they had shared, and the love that he had been lucky enough to have.[3]

Through the use of many such exercises, Frankl began to assert his mental and spiritual freedom. His body was in prison, but his spirit soared beyond it. Through his inner resources, he transcended the walls and fences that held him captive. Ultimately, Frankl survived the prison camp, and rebuilt both his life and his sanity. He founded a very influential school of psychology called "logo therapy," and made seminal contributions to our understanding of human nature. Indeed, the words of the English poet and statesman John Milton are very appropriate here: *The mind is its own place, and in itself can make a heaven of hell, and a hell of heaven.*

When we look at the lives of great men and women, what stands out is their consistent ability to *choose and decide* for themselves, however bad the outside situation may be. Their actions make amply clear the primacy of the inner life, of consciousness, and of self-awareness. As history shows us, even in the most seemingly hopeless situations of overwhelming negativity, individuals have stood up and asserted their freedom. They stand as a testimony to the fact that people can choose their reactions, even in the most degrading of circumstances. As Gandhi told his fellow Indians at the peak of British brutality, *they cannot take our self-respect, if we choose not to give it to them.*

In the last two decades, the corporate world has come to a new understanding. In the past, it was assumed that the wealth of a company lay in its buildings, machinery and other material assets. Companies are now waking up to the reality that the hearts and minds of its employees are its greatest assets, its true competitive advantage. The *New York Times* once stated that the real wealth of Microsoft was in the imagination of its employees. This has been called variously intellectual capital, knowledge capital, etc. Simply put, the things that truly matter are not tangible things at all!

At the time of Gandhi's death, his personal possessions were valued at less than two dollars. He held no property, wealth, office or title. Yet without any material wealth, he accomplished so much. His strength and power was not derived from external things, but rather from the internal depths of his soul. He convincingly demonstrated the supremacy of spiritual power over material possessions. In a world where power is measured by economic wealth and military might, Gandhi showed that the human heart — far from being impotent — is a source of tremendous power that can make possible even the seemingly impossible. It holds the capacity to change the course of history.

12

Choosing Growth over Fear

You need not, and in fact cannot, teach an acorn to grow into an oak tree, but when given a chance, its intrinsic potentialities will develop.[1]

- Karen Homey (1885–1952)

Deep within the recesses of our soul lies a primal urge to rise above our present circumstances, to transcend our limitations. There is an innate tendency within us to learn, grow and mature. Hence, the human heart is always on the lookout for heroes — for great stories, myths, role models and leaders — who inspire, uplift and ennoble us. There is within us the insistent urge towards a greater life, and to go beyond oneself.

In psychology, this innate propensity is towards what has been called self-actualisation, or the capacity for "full humanness."[2] We all hold this tendency to reach out, develop, learn and mature. We move towards increased consciousness and deeper self-awareness. Just as the acorn has an inbuilt propensity towards becoming an oak tree, so do we have an inbuilt potential towards self-actualisation. Western psychology woke up to this fact, thanks to pioneers such as Karen Homey, Carl Rogers (who broke new ground with his "client-centred therapy") and Abraham Maslow (who studied the farther reaches of human nature).

This self-actualisation force or growth tendency is present, to a greater or lesser extent, in all human beings. It manifests itself as an insatiable desire to explore, an unquenchable thirst to know the world and oneself, and an urge to realise our potentials and create a future that is more in sync with our dreams and deepest desires.

The question that immediately arises is why, then, if we all have these potentials — if we *all* possess this urge to grow and transcend — why do so few of us ever make it? Why do so many of us give up on our dreams and surrender to the mundane, ordinary humdrum of everyday existence? Why do so many die with their potentials unrealised and their dreams unlived? As the pioneering American psychologist William James remarked,

> *Compared to what we ought to be, we are only half awake. Our fires are dampened, our drafts are checked, and we are making use of only a small part of our mental and physical resources.*

The answer is that there is another, opposing tendency that exists within us. The yearning to grow exists side-by-side with the equally powerful urge to hold back, and to give in to our fears. There is the tendency within us to prefer safety and security over growth and maturity. We all have (to a greater or lesser extent) a set of mental and emotional tranquilizers such as denial, blind spots, neurosis, justifications, rationalisations and dogma, all of which we use to stay stuck in our regressive behaviours. These two contradictory tendencies of growth and safety operate and coexist within all of us.

The ancient Hindu sages were captivated by the process by which a caterpillar becomes a butterfly. This metamorphosis fascinated them because in this process, they saw a very apt metaphor for human growth and transformation. The caterpillar is protected and nourished within the cocoon and in time, is transformed to become the butterfly. This is an organic, evolutionary process. Amongst human beings, however, it is not quite so simple. On one hand, we want to become a butterfly — we yearn to fulfil our potential. Yet, on the other hand, we are also fearful and we want to stay back in the cocoon that has long since served its purpose. This is the very essence of the human condition: we are torn between safety and growth. We want to flower and blossom and yet, at the same time, we are loath to give up our source of security and prefer to remain an unblossomed bud. This simultaneous existence of the two voices of fear and growth is the source of much of our dilemmas.

So, as human beings, we must choose. All growth and maturity is a dialectic, a dynamic tension between these two opposing tendencies: to stay in our comfort zone, or to take a leap of faith. We can stick to the known, or risk the unknown. Seen from this perspective, life is a series of choices. Almost every day and every hour, we are confronted with making a choice — a crucial decision to progress or regress. We must choose between moving towards safety and moving towards growth. The more we make the choice for growth, the more we move towards self-actualisation.[3] From the cradle to grave, life is one continuous process of making this choice.

The dilemma and the agony of choice between fear and growth stands out most poignantly in the relationship between a patient and a psychotherapist. Let us take the example of John, who is 32 years old, recently married and has been having troubles in his marriage. Although he deeply loves his wife, he is given to sudden bouts of unwarranted anger and is extremely suspicious of his wife's fidelity, even when there is no cause for it. Although married for only a year, both husband and wife are deeply unhappy. John is woefully aware that his current way of living and relating to the world is immature. He knows that he must change, or his marriage could be in jeopardy. He has therefore decided to see a psychotherapist, but since having started therapy, he feels overwhelmed by the level of commitment, risk of openness and amount of honesty that he must bring forth. He has to speak about his unhappy childhood, dredging up painful memories that had been banished to some dark corner of his heart. He is tempted to discontinue therapy, but he stays on. However, he uses all the tricks in the book — denial, rationalisations and excuses — to avoid getting to the issues at hand. He sidesteps key issues that his therapist points out, cancels appointments, turns up late or refuses to do any homework that the therapist suggests.

Here is a situation that is extraordinary, to say the least. On the one hand, it was John's increasing awareness that he had to mature and change that brought him to therapy. This was John choosing the growth option, and making the growth choice. Yet, this is the very same John who is now using all the resources he can muster to avoid that very same growth, maturity and change! John is sabotaging the very change and growth process he had initiated.

At some point in the therapy, there comes a turning point when John, with the help and support of his therapist, finally musters the courage to confront the core issue. He opens up and pours his heart out about his past. Risking pain and vulnerability, he descends to the depths of his heart. He realises that his anger is a cover for his deep feelings of insecurity and fears of abandonment. It is a leftover from his past, where as a child he had not received adequate amounts of love and care from his alcoholic mother. He could never fully feel a bond of trust or a sense of belonging. Also, when John was seven years old, his dad left home and never came back. This abandonment at an early age was fuelling his fears that his wife might leave him too, and hence he constantly doubted her fidelity. Through many such painful but ultimately healing sessions, John emerges a more self-aware person. He attempts to work on his marriage with these newly-won insights. The therapy proceeds towards successful completion.

John's impulse to evolve and mature prevailed over his fears and doubts. But, as psychologists will tell you, in many cases, this does not happen. Patients discontinue therapy suddenly, and they succumb to their fears and find it overwhelming to step out of their cocoon. Although John is a fictional example and his story simplistic, it is a broad, general outline of what goes on in many successful therapy situations. Actual situations tend to be much more subtle, complex and nuanced than this example, but it highlights the choice between growth and fear that every human being must ultimately make.

People who live a life of significance and worth — people who make a positive and long-standing contribution to the world — have chosen to follow the self that desires growth, maturity, learning and creativity, rather than the self that is fearful of growth and wants to stay behind. They move forward and choose the growth option, *in spite of* their fear. Gandhi was a very shy and fearful child, but from his mid-twenties onwards, he consciously and consistently chose the growth option. He chose to progress rather than regress. He risked failure, explored, experimented and learnt from his mistakes. He took up rather than avoided responsibility. He attempted to practice what he had studied in books written by Tolstoy, Thoreau and Ruskin, the Bhagavad-Gita and the Sermon on the Mount, and he proactively chose the right role models. Gandhi writes that with any new task or responsibility, he would accept in "fear and trembling"—but accept them he did, because he chose to follow the growth impulse rather than the fear impulse.

13

Stewardship: The Urge to Serve

I don't know what your destiny will be, but one thing I do know: the only ones among you who will be really happy are those who have sought and found how to serve.

- Albert Schweitzer (1875–1965)

We are all brought up with the very seductive illusion that we are only driven by our own narrow self-interests, and that it's "each man for himself" in this "dog eat dog" world. This has been the dominant paradigm of the business world, and the world in which we have grown up. Yet, what we forget or neglect is that we all have a deep-rooted desire to serve, to care for, and to tend to others. According to Shelley Taylor, a psychology professor at UCLA, tending and caring for others is as natural and biologically based as eating or sleeping, and it originates from deep within our social nature. She writes in her groundbreaking book *The Tending Instinct* that we are primarily a "nurturant species."[1]

Extraordinary human beings like Gandhi, Mother Teresa and Albert Schweitzer all consciously set out to develop this urge. In fact, most of us engage in small and great acts of kindness with our friends, acquaintances and even strangers quite regularly. But the greats make it into a conscious, sustained effort. As Gandhi writes,

Consciously, or unconsciously, every one of us does render some service or other. If we cultivate the

97

habit of doing this service deliberately, our desire for service will steadily grow stronger, and will make not only for our own happiness, but that of the world at large.[2]

Even as a young boy, Gandhi loved nursing and often tended to his sick father. In South Africa, he volunteered to help out at the local hospital. During times of war, he brought together nursing units that could help the wounded, risking his life and limb at the front lines. He then helped many illiterate, indentured labourers without expecting fees from them. By indulging regularly in this passion to serve, Gandhi consciously developed this tendency, and by the time he came back to India to help in the freedom struggle, he had indulged his passion to serve so regularly that serving and caring became the central theme of his life.

Studies suggest that helping others has a healing/beneficial effect on both the helped and the helper. This phenomenon has been well documented by research and it even has a name: "helper's high."[3]

Psychologist David McClelland at Harvard University did an interesting study in which he showed to students a film of Mother Teresa caring for the sick. He measured the students' salivary IgA levels before and after the film. All those who viewed the film showed noticeable immune function improvement. Irrespective of whether people said they liked her or disliked her, all those who watched the film showed an increase in their IgA levels (IgA is an antibody in the saliva which protects against colds and other respiratory infections). This study indicates that in spite of our everyday, superficial beliefs, the deeper parts of our consciousness seem to be predisposed to tender, loving care, and we respond to it even when we are only a distant, observing third party.[4]

Psychologist Martin Seligman conducted an informal study wherein he asked his students to perform one altruistic act (such as helping somebody) and one pleasurable act (such as indulging in one's favourite food). The students all reported an inner glow from the altruistic act that lasted long after the gratification from the pleasurable act had vanished.[5]

These studies, among many others, seem to suggest that not only do we all have a deep-seated yearning to tend to and care for others, but that such caring and tending to others is also physically, mentally and emotionally nourishing to all involved.

Nobel Laureate and celebrated Indian poet Rabindranath Tagore tells us of the following experience he had as a child. In his memoirs, he writes of a young man named Hammargren, who had travelled from Sweden to India. This young man, upon his arrival in Calcutta, chose to live amidst the poorest of the poor, and freely offered and bestowed his help to all. He would earn his money teaching French and German to the rich people of Calcutta, and then use that money to help the poor children buy books for school. His dream was to build a library for these children, and hence he would try to save as much of his earnings as he could. In fact, he was so eager to save money and help the children that he avoided transport and walked to work — often for many miles, in the harsh Indian sun. Tagore writes that he was deeply moved by such "reckless generosity of love": the young man helped, served and tended to the poor with a deep sense of humility. Such a display of loving kindness and sensitivity evoked within Tagore "feelings of love bordering on awe."

Unfortunately, the young man died with his dream unfulfilled; the library could not be built. The strain of having to live in an alien culture, combined with the harsh Indian climate, finally took its toll. He had been completely spent, and died amidst the very poor of the land, far away from his home. Writes Tagore,

We all have a realm, a private paradise, in our mind, where dwell deathless memories of persons who brought some divine light to our life's experience, who may not be known to others, and whose names have no place in the pages in the history. Let me confess to you that this man lives as one of those immortals in the paradise of my individual life.[6]

Such stories of service and altruism are deeply moving to us, because we all feel this empathy towards others, and this urge to serve. There are many such Hammargrens whose names are lost to history, and such stories do not get reported. Our society, for the most part, has focused almost fanatically on man's selfish nature and the "what's in it for me?" mentality. We end up thinking that human nature is narrowly self-centred or aimed only toward the pursuit of power and aggression.

In the Indian tradition of Yoga, service to others is a legitimate and powerful path to spiritual enlightenment, and this path is called "karma yoga." All the world's great wisdom traditions have recognised charity, altruism and serving others as an integral element of one's spiritual growth and maturity. Psychologists also agree that serving and volunteering is healthy, because it enables us to step out of our preoccupation with our problems and issues, and allows us to empathise with others. It makes us more fully human, by opening us up and connecting us with joys and sorrows, and both the beauty and sadness of the world. It makes us whole. It is indeed very revealing that the words "heal" and "whole" share the same root word.

Robert Greenleaf wrote a book called *Servant Leadership*, in which he first put forward the idea that truly great leaders are always, first and foremost, servants.[7] This is obvious to some, but it seems like a radical idea in our day and age. Many of those who are passed off as leaders today are those who are primarily driven by a thirst for power, and those who want to aggrandise and accumulate at any cost. However, the true, effective leader is a *servant leader* who is motivated by a genuine urge to serve — driven by a loving empathy, rather than a desire for personal glory.

One of the problems with such cliches and platitudes as "dare to be different" and "go your own way" is that they place an exclusive focus on individuality. This individuality, in order to be healthy, must be balanced by a concern for others. Without this concern, individuality degenerates into selfishness and an obsession with the self. Those who dare to be different, for the mere sake of *being* different, may achieve notoriety and infamy, but those things soon fade away. In the process, "going your own way" becomes an excuse to justify one's selfishness. The ones whose names endure — those who, like Gandhi, leave behind a lasting legacy — invest their energies, talents and skills to making a positive contribution to the lives of others.

When we study the lives of people such as Gandhi, Mother Teresa or Albert Schweitzer, we see that they made a positive difference in their own lives by making a difference in other people's lives. As Gandhi wrote, "The best way to find yourself is to lose yourself in the service of others." The core question that they all seemed to have asked is how can I put my skills, talents and abilities in the service of others?

14

Beyond Competition

So far as man is concerned, if competition, in its aggressive combative sense, ever had any adaptive value among men, which is to be greatly doubted, it is quite clear that it has no adaptive value whatever in the modern world. Perhaps never before in the history of man has there been so high a premium upon the adaptive value of cooperative behavior.[1]

Ashley Montagu, Darwin:
Competition and Cooperation

Many of us have the deeply-held view that life equals competition. We are socially conditioned to see a world where competition is inevitable. We have grown up in a competitive world, and we have witnessed the triumph of narrow self-interest in schools, in the workplace, and in the wider world around us. This has hence become our "normal" mode of thinking and living. Thus, we come to implicitly believe that life is a "zero sum game," where success for some requires that some others fail. We are conditioned by a social system that teaches us to triumph over others, and even to view them as obstacles to our own success. We see others not as potential friends, but rivals. This cherished illusion — that competition is inevitable — has become a taken-for-granted truth. But our obsession with competition is a self-fulfilling prophecy: the world is so competitive because we make it that way. As a society, we routinely overestimate the strengths of competition, and underestimate the power of co-operation.

In his book, *No Contest: The Case Against Competition*, Alfie Kohn brings together research from social scientists, biologists, psychologists and social psychologists to show that there is *no* overwhelming evidence proving that competition is innate or a part of human nature. In fact, research suggests that it is not innate but learned.[2] It *seems* natural, but only because our social structures and institutions perpetuate and reinforce it. The reason why we hold on to this cherished notion is because the world of "business" intrudes into virtually every aspect of our lives. Business corporations derive many of its models, metaphors and ways of functioning from the arena of sports (where competition is necessary) or the military (where the concept of the enemy exists). But life is larger than business. There is much more to life than competition.

When we look at the lives of people such as Gandhi, Buddha, Rumi, William Blake, Emerson, Thoreau and Mother Teresa, we can, without hesitation, apply the term "great" to all of them, and yet competition — or the competitive spirit — was remarkably absent amongst all of them. In fact, we could say that they tended towards the *opposite*: cooperation. Their lives show that exemplary character can be built without the competitive spirit, and in the process they shatter the myth that competition is necessary to achieving excellence in a field. They achieved distinction and path-breaking creativity not through competition, but in the absence of it!

This is not a recommendation to do away with competition, but rather for us to realise that life is about much more than competition — tremendously more. A life aimed merely at beating others and crushing the competition may work in the short term, but it seldom leads to greatness. There is more to life than status, rankings and ratings. Competition or competing with others may at times be unavoidable or even necessary (especially within sports or business), and valuable lessons may be learned therein, but it is not an end towards which a fulfilling life is directed.

Even within business and sports, it is not all about competition. In fact, in order to compete and excel in the world of sports or business, there has to be a high level of collaboration, support and cooperation *within* the team. The team members have to bond at some level so that there is trust, which allows them to work in sync with each other. Teams that consistently perform well usually have individual members who display not only a high level of self-awareness but also a greater level of "group consciousness". Phil Jackson, one of the most successful coaches in American Basket Ball history (NBA) writes in his book, *Sacred Hoops* that winning at the highest level and winning consistently requires, among other things, the individual to surrender his or her narrow self-interest for the greater good of the team. Every player in the team must play through selfless teamwork — by putting the "we" ahead of the "me."[3] This is, according to him, one of the core qualities of a great team and is what allows a team to win on a regular basis. On the other hand, when a team is ego- dominated where players are merely worried only about their individual scores and see others in the team as competitive threats, there may be great individual performances, but that team will seldom be able to scale the heights collectively. This holds true not just within the world of sports but also within the world of business.

In fact, the exclusive emphasis on competition and "winning at all costs" often leads to crises of ethics. An exclusively "bottom line"-oriented culture breeds corruption. The business world has recently been rocked by scandals within companies such as Enron, WorldCom, and Arthur Andersen, among many others. Executives within these companies resorted to cheating and lying. They forged papers, shredded documents, embellished accounting figures and lied to their stakeholders, all because winning and beating the competition became so important. In the end these companies collapsed, and millions of people have suffered in the form of lost jobs or retirement resources.

Howard Schultz, the CEO and cofounder of Starbucks, wrote a book called *Pour Your Heart Into It: How Starbucks Built a Company One Step at a Time*. In it, he tells the story of how Starbucks grew from its small Seattle roots to an international organisation with over 2,000 stores. In this book, Schultz hardly mentions anything about the competition; in fact, fewer than three pages of this 340-page book are devoted to the competition. Instead, in page after page, he speaks of his passion for great coffee, his ambition to build a great company, his joy in seeing satisfied customers and his love of working with people who share his vision.[4] For a company that brought in net revenues of close to $1 billion in 1997 (when CEO Howard Schultz wrote the book) and is still growing quite strongly, the relative lack of discussion on competition is remarkable. In this sense, Schultz belongs in the same category as other visionary leaders who do not make "beating the competition" their primary motivation or mandate.

When we overvalue competition and undervalue cooperation, we are sending the message to our children that competition is greater than cooperation, when in fact the reverse is true. Finding effective solutions to the problems and challenges faced by the human race in the 21st century, requires that we all cooperate not compete. Cooperation is the way forward because it takes note of the interdependent nature of all life.

15

Religion: An Invitation to Think

Let knowledge come to us from all directions.

- Rig Veda

Gandhi read the spiritual books and valued the wisdom of the elders. He looked to them for spiritual insight and guidance. However, he also used his own faculties of objectivity, thinking, reasoning and reflecting. He adopted only those principles, religious values and ethics that he felt were right, and which were tried and tested in his own life through personal experience and experiments. To Gandhi, authentic religion or spirituality was *an invitation to start thinking, and not an excuse to stop thinking.*

The Buddha said to his followers,

> *Believe nothing. No matter where you read it, or who said it, even if I have said it unless it agrees with your own reason and your own common sense... Be a lamp unto yourselves.*

Gandhi did exactly that. He attempted to learn from books, spiritual masters, guides and mentors. But he did not stop there. He also learnt through his personal encounters, through relationships. He learnt by observing, examining, experimenting, testing and reflecting on the experiences and events of his life. He made full use of his inner forces of awareness and consciousness. In Gandhi's opinion, if one were truly a seeker who sought after truth, one would try to learn from *all* available sources. As a seeker, he maintained an unceasingly open approach in his search.

Unfortunately, many people who call themselves "religious" are simply satisfied to be spectators, unquestioningly accepting the codes and canons of their religions and pledging their blind allegiance to it. In religious matters, they become too exclusively dependent on outside authorities and institutions. The difficult and painful process of wrestling with their selves and their consciences is one they would rather avoid than confront. By thus simply settling for secondhand knowledge, religion becomes an excuse to *stop* thinking. This is sometimes precipitated by the religious institutions themselves, which often attempt to smother reflection and stifle open and critical dialogue. However, a truly growing, learning and maturing individual will not be blindly obedient to religious authorities or books, nor will they unquestioningly accept everything that they are told in a church, synagogue, temple, or mosque. Rather, they will deeply reflect upon and accept something only if it agrees with their reason, intuition and common sense. In an individual of increasing self-awareness, we see a dialectic — a dynamic tension between the wisdom of the books and the wisdom within.

Gandhi attempted to learn from all sources. Apart from regularly spending time in reflection, he read the Bhagavad-Gita on regular basis. He also read the Sermon on the Mount and the Koran. He had discussions with Christians, Jews and Muslims on spiritual, philosophical and practical issues. According to Gandhi, the spiritual texts, mentors and spiritual guides can all complement and supplement us in our spiritual growth. But they cannot be substitutes for this journey. Nobody else can make the journey for us. We have to learn through personal experience, by paying the price of undergoing this process of inner wrestling.

16

Inclusivity

An individual has not started living until he can rise above the narrow confines of individualistic concerns to the broader concerns of all humanity.

- Martin Luther King, Jr. (1929–1968)

A significant discovery in developmental psychology has been that the growing, aware, mature individual develops an ever-widening circle of compassion. Highly self-aware individuals such as Gandhi show an increasing sense of care, concern and compassion beyond the borders of their family and friends. Kindness and charity do begin at home, but it should not end there. As their compassion grows, it embraces and encompasses a larger group of people: those beyond their tribe, their culture and their country. In their best moments, they become concerned with all of humanity.

For all of us, our childhood starts as a preoccupation with the self. Childhood, to a very large extent, is marked by narcissism. It is an essential part of the growth process. Slowly, the growing child steps out of this narcissism by developing a concern for family and close friends. As the child matures into a healthy adult, he or she begins to exhibit a concern for the community, and the tribe. Finally, if the individual grows and matures further, this concern evolves to nature, to the world at large — beyond the borders of culture, religion, country or tribal group. As philosopher Ken Wilber explains, ideal growth unfolds in the following manner: from *me* to *us* to *all of us*. Hence, growth and maturity can be seen as moving along a continuum, from *selfish* to *care* to *universal care.*[1]

Growth implies a rising beyond our tribal consciousness, There is a healthier part of us that drives us towards greater unity and a sense of ever-increasing kinship with the world at large. Spiritual philosophers point out that the family does not limit us in our love, but rather it is a first inkling, a signpost that teaches us of our intricate connection with the rest of the world. It is a preparation for greater things to come. As Gandhi grew and matured, his empathy and compassion were not limited to the few people close to him, but rather continued to expand and become ever more inclusive and enlightened. He began to exhibit a growing sense of fairness, care and concern for people and issues far beyond the borders of his immediate family or clan. He began to look at issues through the lens of a *shared humanity.*

The wisdom traditions of the world mention that all men are brothers. The highest truth as proclaimed by all the mystics, saints, sages, and spiritual philosophers is this: ultimately, there is no "they." There is only us, "all of us." Exclusivist thinking is an ignorance of the deeper truth and the common bond that exists between others and us. We are constantly looking at life through the lens of "us vs. them." The deeper one delves as self-awareness increases, the more one is capable of seeing this underlying bond, this deeper unity. Differences and uniqueness are not negated, but beneath it all, one will grow to notice an underlying common thread. In fact, in the spiritual wisdom of the east, spiritual growth is the increasing ability to see this underlying unity among all things on the planet. The great Albert Einstein would agree with this wholeheartedly; he writes very eloquently about our "task" as human beings:

A human being is a part of a whole, called by us —
[the] universe... He experiences himself, his thoughts
and feelings as something separated from the rest...
a kind of optical delusion of his consciousness. This
delusion is a kind of prison for us, restricting us to our
personal desires and to affection for a few persons
nearest to us. Our task must be to free ourselves from
this prison by widening our circle of compassion to
embrace all living creatures and the whole of nature
in its beauty.

One of the charges levelled against religious institutions has
been that they have been the cause for wars, of preaching
exclusivity and intolerance towards others. When one looks
at history, it would be hard to argue the fact that religious
institutions have played a role in instigating intolerance
and violence against people of other religions and faiths.
But every religion or spiritual tradition has also brought
forth many great men and women who have attempted to
bring humanity *together*, rather than tear them apart. They
preached and embodied a profound tolerance and respect for
each other's differences, because they noted the underlying
unity of all beings. As the philosopher sage Emerson
exhorted, *Be ye an opener of doors.* The best among us
have tended towards inclusivity, not exclusivity; they have
been bridge builders, door openers and wall breakers. They
have aimed to connect, not isolate — and of course, among
them is Gandhi, who wrote that

We must widen the circle of our love till it embraces
the whole village; the village in its turn must take into
its fold the district, the district the province, and so
on till the scope of our love becomes co-terminus with
the world.[2]

17

The Power of Conscience

Nothing is at last sacred but the integrity of your own mind.

- Ralph Waldo Emerson (1803–1882)

Many philosophers of yore — including mystics, saints and sages — have affirmed that we human beings are endowed with an innate moral sense. While a child may not arrive into the world with a fully-formed moral sense, conscience begins to manifest itself as the individual matures to adulthood. We all have what is called a "conscience," although some of us hear its voice much more clearly than do others. A well-developed conscience is like an inner navigational system — a highly intelligent guidance mechanism that helps us weigh the issues of right and wrong, wrestle with moral and ethical dilemmas, and ultimately choose the right way to live. Ralph Waldo Emerson called it the "blessed impulse," or the "primary wisdom." Gandhi alluded to it as the "still small voice within." We are seldom quiet enough or peaceful enough to be in touch with this voice, but most of us are aware of its existence within.

Our social and cultural milieu, our religious upbringing, our educational system — all this and more impacts us in a million different ways. By the time we stand at the threshold of adulthood, we have been influenced, shaped and moulded to an extraordinary extent. Hence we all begin life with a "borrowed set of standards." While much of this is essential and good, we inevitably also inherit many unquestioned rules of living, prejudices and dogmas. We live in society, but more importantly, society *lives in us.*

We learn through our culture, our parents and significant elders, and institutions. But as we grow older, at some point, growth and maturity requires transcending the views and assumptions of our culture, family, profession and socio-economic class. This is a vital requirement for the full flowering of our conscience. While childhood and the teen years is a time during which one is "programmed" and conditioned, adulthood should ideally be a time to critically examine those "programs" given to us by our parents, peers, culture and social institutions. To consciously think, reflect upon, and choose a set of independent standards and values is the most crucial assignment of adulthood. Through self-awareness, *we examine the examiner:* our paradigms, taken-for-granted assumptions, norms, customs, internal scripts and maps.

The lives of great people such as Gandhi hold a critical lesson for us here. Like all human beings, Gandhi was shaped and conditioned by the social and cultural milieu of both his time and society. He was born into a Hindu family in 1870s India, belonging to the Vaishya caste. But Gandhi's growth did not stop there. As he began to grow in self-awareness, he went beyond the cultural and social programming of his time; he did not blindly *accept everything* that his culture and religion taught him. He consciously reflected, introspected, and accepted what he felt deep down to be right and rejected what he felt was morally and ethically wrong.

Many of us, unfortunately, come to accept the ideas and assumptions of our society or our tribe as "givens" that are set in stone. When this happens, our authentic inner voice of conscience is subdued or is mistaken for conformity to one's country, society, religion, etc. As social psychologists such as Erich Fromm point out, many people think they act in accordance with their conscience, but in reality they may be blindly mirroring their society's standards of good and bad or right and wrong.[1] They deem something "normal" and accepted, merely because their society considers it "normal."

Take, as an example, the issue of slavery. Today, most of us are abhorrent of the very word, because we clearly know it is wrong. But in the past, throughout the many years in which slavery was practiced, it was considered "normal" and even approved by God. In practicing and/or supporting slavery, these men and women felt that they were acting in accordance with the voice of their conscience. As we can see now, however, they were blindly mirroring the dominant values and attitudes of their society, and *mistaking it for* their conscience. Most people went about their business as if this was "normal." It was only a few — a distinct minority — who at that time felt deeply that slavery was wrong. Even fewer dared to speak out against it.

How do we develop the ability to hear this authentic inner voice and learn to differentiate it from the internalised voice of our parents, society or culture? We can learn from Gandhi's life: he ceaselessly sought to listen to and develop his conscience, all by reflecting and contemplating on his experiences. Gandhi regularly examined his life, his experiences, his standards and his values. He observed one day of silence per week, spent time with nature, and spun a charka — the last of which, for Gandhi, was also a form of meditation. In this way, he cultivated his inner peace and could thus listen to his conscience with greater clarity. He created an environment around him that was conducive to the maturity of his conscience and character. In doing so, he inadvertently answered the call of Marcus Aurelius, who said, *look within. Within is the fountain of good, and it will ever bubble up, if you will ever dig.*

Gandhi also took risks by exposing himself to new situations, people and experiences. The young Gandhi travelled to England to study when he was 18 years old. This was back in the 1890s when travelling overseas was very uncommon, and especially so for Indians. Although it was daunting for the young man to learn a new language and to adjust to new food, new customs and a different culture, this exposure broadened his horizons. Similarly, Gandhi leapt at the chance to go to South Africa when he was 24 years old. In both England and South Africa, Gandhi mixed and mingled with Christians, Jews, Muslims, Indians, South Africans and Britons. By thus coming into regular contact with diverse points of view and belief systems and worldviews different from his own, Gandhi began to question and reflect on his taken-for-granted assumptions. Not only did he begin to question his own religion and culture, but he also questioned each and every one of these other cultures and religions. Apart from learning something valuable from all these cultures and religions, he arrived at a deeper, more inclusive and more holistic understanding of the world and of himself. It enabled him to identify with all of humanity, irrespective of colour, creed, religion or nationality.

Many of us spend a lot of time with people who think in ways similar to us. This only reinforces our biases and prejudices, and from it we gain a false sense of certainty about our ideas and views, hence making them appear to us as infallible. There is sense of "safety in numbers," and in the presence of likeminded people, we are less likely to question the validity and correctness of our ideas and assumptions. There is a great price we pay for this: we stunt our own growth and remain the proverbial "frogs in the well" who assume the "well" to be the whole world. What truly gives us an inner conviction is the questioning and examining of our paradigms, our assumptions and experiences, and trying to expand our horizons.

By thus developing his conscience, Gandhi became the conscious architect of his life, rather than being passively designed by his childhood experiences. He did not simply live out the borrowed scripts of the past. When he was exposed to new ideas, people and experiences — and later reflected on these experiences — there was a gradual change in the way he saw himself and the world. He was thus able to rise above the *hypnosis of social conditioning.*

18

The Importance of Courage

*Conscience tells us what is right and what is wrong.
But it is our courage that will move us to speak out
and take action even if it means risking our very life.
For conscience to be truly effective, courage must be
present.*

Gandhi realised that there was a crucial relationship between courage and conscience. Without courage, conscience will not translate into effective action. It takes courage to act according to our conscience, for doing so can often make us unpopular, even within our own group. Studies have overwhelmingly shown that group membership and how the group views a person is very important to many people. We will go to great lengths to conform, and hence create and maintain a positive social image. It takes special courage to speak out against something that our conscience tells us is wrong, especially if people around us do not see it the same way.

Gandhi, for example, knew very clearly that "untouchability" was wrong. In fact, he found it abhorrent to his whole being. The caste system, according to historians and Indology experts, seems to have originated as a social classification system that could enable the smoother functioning of society. It created the castes of the Brahmins (the intellectual class), the Kshatriyas (the warrior class), the Vaishyas (the trader class, to which Gandhi belonged), and the Shudras (the service and labour class). It was a practice that had become entrenched in the Indian psyche over many centuries, and whatever its original meaning and intent, the fact is that it devolved with the passage of time into something grotesque. Entire groups of people, by mere reason of birth, were condemned to humiliation, discrimination and social and economic hardships. These groups of people were regarded as "untouchable" by people of the higher castes. It was considered "polluting" for a high-caste person to even go near *the shadow of* an "untouchable" person.

Gandhi knew that, he would have to take on the powerful Hindu orthodoxy. He was courageous enough to speak out for the abolition of "untouchability," for which there was initially a tremendous backlash against Gandhi. Many orthodox Hindus were outraged. But he took a decisive, vital step and unwaveringly fought the system. At one point, funding for his ashram was withdrawn because Gandhi had allowed a lower-caste family to stay there. Still, Gandhi refused to back down. He risked unpopularity, ostracism, serious damage to reputation, and even death. Gandhi stood his ground resolutely, and refused to go into temples that had closed its doors to "untouchables." He made it a rule in his ashrams and farms that there would be complete equality, and he worked tirelessly for the social and economic betterment of these people.

In this cause, Gandhi even resorted to his "infallible weapon" — fasting. He decided to fast unto death for this cause. In a statement issued on the eve of the fast he stated, *if the Hindu mass mind is not yet prepared to banish untouchability root and branch it must sacrifice me without the slightest hesitation.* He sought to sting the conscience of the people into right action, and it worked: the news that Gandhi was about to fast shook Indians from coast to coast. A: the fast progressed and Gandhi's health began to rapidly deteriorate, there was a tremendous outpouring of emotion. All across India, and even in some of the most orthodox states, temples, wells and public places were thrown open to the "untouchables." In a symbolic gesture, women from the high castes accepted food from the "untouchables." Letters began to pour in to Gandhi, pleading him to stop the fast; they promised that they would reform their ways. On the sixth day, Gandhi ended his fast.

After this, Gandhi embarked on a countrywide tour, covering 12,500 miles and lasting for nine months. During this tour, he exhorted his countrymen to erase the blot of "untouchability." Gandhi was received with great enthusiasm throughout this tour, but it also provoked the ire of the orthodox Hindus. There was an assassination attempt on his life as a bomb was thrown. (Fortunately, Gandhi was unhurt.) Still, Gandhi did not waver.

By consistently appealing to the higher nature within people — their better instincts, he was able to change many people's minds and hearts about the horrendous nature of "untouchability." Although Gandhi could not completely abolish the practice of untouchability, he nevertheless made a huge dent in this custom that had developed over many centuries. His fasting and exhortations rendered it "morally illegitimate."[1] Today, social workers and humanitarian organisations continue to build on the legacy left by Gandhi in this area.

Martin Luther King, Jr., leader of the civil rights movement in America, similarly stood up for his conscience. During the Vietnam War, King was one of the first few who openly criticised the American Government for its actions in Vietnam. There was a time when King became very unpopular in his country, and he became a lightening rod for anger and criticism. Even his closest supporters were angry that he was wasting time on an issue that did not seem to be connected with the civil rights struggle. But King continued to speak out strongly against the Vietnam War and in so doing he risked disapproval. In reply to his critics, he stated that he could not segregate his moral concern, or his "field of moral vision." In his own words, "Justice is indivisible. Injustice anywhere is a threat to justice everywhere"[2]. He stated unequivocally that he would take up a stand against injustice, whether it happened in America or in Vietnam.

Most of us lack the courage to stand up for our beliefs and values. We are very scared of ostracism. Although we know clearly that certain things are wrong, and although our sense of justice and fairness is violated, we do not say much for fear of tainting our social image, or of losing our friends and social status. Although we sympathise with a cause and are touched by the injustice meted out to our fellow beings, this sympathy does not always translate into effective action. In the words of Annie Besant (1847– 1933), a theosophist and women's rights activist,

> *Plenty of people wish well to any good cause; but very few care to exert themselves to help it, and still fewer will risk anything in its support. "Some one ought to do it, but why should I? " is the ever reechoed phrase of weak-kneed amiability. "Some one ought to do it, so why not I? " is the cry of some earnest servant of man, eagerly forward springing to face some perilous duty. Between these two sentences lie whole centuries of moral evolution.*

The most dramatic and stirring example of conscience and courage comes from Socrates (469–399 BC), a Greek philosopher from Athens who preferred death rather than betray his conscience. Socrates' view was that philosophy was the necessary pursuit of all intelligent persons. Socrates practiced philosophy in the truest sense of the word: the word "philosophy" comes from two Greek words (*Philo* meaning love, and *Sophia*, the Greek goddess of wisdom), and so philosophy was for him the very *love of wisdom*. He dedicated himself to this search, and became a guide to his fellow Athenians in their intellectual, moral and spiritual development. He spent his days discussing ideas, ideals and values such as virtue, justice, and freedom wherever his fellow citizens congregated. This upset many of those in power; he was brought to trial for corrupting youth and for religious heresies. He was forced to leave Athens or face death. He could have lived in exile, but leaving Athens would imply that everything he stood for and had taught was wrong. Stating that "the unexamined life is not worth living," Socrates bravely chose death rather than compromise his principles.

The crucial lesson we learn from all these examples is that while conscience helps us distinguish right from wrong, it is our *courage* that enables us to speak out and take action against injustice and cruelty. It is courage that makes it possible to stand up for what we believe in.

19

The Salt March and the Calcutta Fast

In this chapter, we pause and take a break from outlining the lessons from Gandhi's life. Before proceeding any further, it would be appropriate to study in greater detail, two seminal events in the life of Gandhi. These two events, The Salt March of 1930 and The Calcutta Miracle of 1947 go down in history as two of Gandhi's finest moments and they will give us a deeper understanding of what Gandhi stood for and the power of the Satyagraha movement pioneered by him.

The Dandi March

In 1915, when Gandhi returned from South Africa and started to lead the Indian independence movement, he was open to the idea of dominion status for India, similar to what Australia and Canada had earlier gained. Britain, however, would have none of it; it refused to relax her stranglehold on the Indian colony. In the 15 years that Gandhi had been in India, Britain's repression and subjugation was only worsening. Gandhi now knew that dominion status would not do; India would need complete independence from an empire that was becoming increasingly evil.

On January 1, 1930, the Indian National Congress defiantly unfurled a flag of "free India." It was done to serve as a powerful symbol that India wanted complete independence, and that now she would struggle and strain with all her might to achieve it. The nation was restless, with everybody waiting and watching with bated breath. The youth around the country were beginning to get impatient and edgy. They hitherto had not believed in the efficacy of Gandhi's methods, dismissing him as a "silly old fool," and a "saint who cannot lead us." They increasingly realised, however, that Gandhi was the man for the job. Letters from men, women and even children were beginning to pour into Sabarmati Ashram, where Gandhi was staying. They wanted action — decisive action — and they were eager to help.

Gandhi withdrew and cloistered himself, turning his searchlight within. He spent his days in prayer, silence and spinning the charka. He waited for an answer from within. Were his countrymen ready? Were they ready to undergo the tough suffering that any decisive action would involve? Were they disciplined enough not to retaliate when the British would inevitably resort to violence? India was a nation divided along the multiple lines of caste, religion, community, economic wealth and state loyalties. What could get everybody "on board"? Most of his earlier campaigns had been done within a particular region, but now the whole nation was watching and waiting.

By the end of February 1930, he had the answer. The British had imposed a steep tax on salt and Gandhi drawing on all his past experiences and experiments, developed a plan and strategy. The plan was that he and 78 of his fellow ashram members would march to the coastal town of Dandi, 240 kilometres away, and pick up salt from the shoreline, thus technically breaking the law. This would then serve as a signal for the entire nation to disobey the salt law — and it would serve as a clarion call for a larger, nationwide civil disobedience campaign.

When Gandhi announced his plan, even his closest aides and associates were completely unconvinced. The Indian

National Congress was mystified and incredulous. Of all things, why *salt*? Gandhi had once again proved that he was no mere saint-like figure, but also a superb strategist. This would prove to be his masterstroke, as it was a plan that was at once simple and brilliant. Salt, for Gandhi, was largely symbolic; by choosing salt as an issue, Gandhi was showcasing the heartlessness of an empire that would tax something so basic and essential to the human diet. It served as a powerful symbol of the callous and cruel colonial exploitation, imposing a burden on the already-poor millions. What was even more ridiculous was that salt could be freely made on the seashores, yet no Indian was allowed to make it. If ever a law could be unjust, here was one. Above all, given the essential nature of its use, this issue would cut across all lines of caste, creed, state and language. Finally, it was a powerful emotional issue for the Indian woman struggling to feed her family.

Gandhi then wrote a letter to the British viceroy of India, addressing the letter as "Dear Friend." (This was always a part of the Gandhian method; in his worldview, there were no enemies, because he was fighting the evil of the system and not these individuals. He hated the sin, but not the sinner.) He fully informed the viceroy of the plan, and detailed the reasons of why the campaign was necessary; he wrote of how the actions of the empire had left him and his followers with no choice. He fully disclosed his plans and wrote that he did not intend to spring any behind-the-back surprises, and that everything would be done in full view.

On March 30, 1930, the day of the event, an immense crowd had gathered outside the ashram. There was a tremendous energy of excitement and expectation. After prayers and chanting, Gandhi, along with 78 ashram members, set off for the village of Dandi, 240 miles away. They walked briskly along the dusty roads of India, on a clear sunny day, with crowds cheering, clapping and egging them on. They stopped at villages on the way, resting and holding prayer meetings. This was again a part of the Gandhian strategy, to help build momentum and allow time for the news media (both Indian and International) to arrive on the scene; they came in large numbers. Villagers flocked to catch a glimpse of this remarkable little brown man. Many joined the rally, and the size was increasing with each passing day. A number of fellow marchers grew tired and rode on bullock carts for a while to rest their sore feet and gather their energy. Not so with Gandhi. He was 61 and was marching along, determined. He knew that here was an idea whose time had come; it was, in his words, "an opportunity of a lifetime." He wanted to show to the world that non-violence was a powerful weapon in the momentous "battle of Right versus Might." Years later, Nehru, Gandhi's protégé, would write,

> *Many pictures rise in my mind of this man [Gandhi]....*
> *But the picture that is dominant... is as I saw him*
> *marching, staff in hand, to Dandi on the salt march*
> *in 1930. Here was the pilgrim on his quest of Truth,*
> *quiet, peaceful, determined and fearless, who would*
> *continue that quest and pilgrimage, regardless of*
> *consequences.* [1]

They had been marching for 24 days. What had started as a group of 78 swelled to several thousand people, the entourage now two miles long as they headed close to the seaside of Dandi. They reached the seaside of Dandi in the evening. Gandhi stated that the salt law would be broken on the next day. The day chosen was not random: it was on this day, 10 years previous, that 340 men and women had been killed at a religious gathering. They had been brutally shot in cold blood by General Dyer and his troops.

There was an all-night vigil, with a prayer meeting under the stars. Morning came and this sea of humanity, led by Gandhi and representing the hopes and yearnings of all Indians, made its way to the sea. Gandhi paused, bent down and picked up a few grains of salt from the seashore, and held it up. It was a symbolic gesture that meant that the law was now to be broken. The crowd erupted in a frenzy of joy. All the Indians present lined up the seashore and began to make salt, thus breaking the law.

The news of Dandi spread like wildfire across the country, and people all over India's vast coastline began breaking the salt law. Initially, the British had been ambivalent about arresting Gandhi, because they did not want to further arouse the passions of the people. But they had seriously miscalculated. People across the nation, inspired by the events at Dandi, were joining in the civil disobedience, breaking the law and quietly courting arrest without resorting to violence. The fire unleashed at Dandi was sweeping across the nation.

A brutal reprisal followed as the British tried to break up the crowds. They arrested all the top leaders of the independence movement. They filled the prisons with an unprecedented 60,000 people. Nonetheless, the movement showed no signs of abating. The British forces could not stem the tide. Nehru writes about how astonished he was to see salt transforming into such a "mysterious word" — a symbol of such power that seemed to unite all Indians. He recalls,

It seemed as though a spring had been released...
As we saw the abounding enthusiasm of the people
and the way salt-making was spreading like a prairie
fire, we felt a little abashed and ashamed for having
questioned the efficacy of this method when it was
first proposed by Gandhiji. And we marvelled at the

amazing knack of the man to impress the multitude
and make it act in an organized way.²

The remarkable and unprecedented events of Dandi culminated at the Darsana salt works. Gandhi was now in prison, but another protégé of Gandhi, Sarojini Naidu, led a group of 2,500 volunteers and satyagrahis in a non-violent raid into the salt works. The volunteers were prepared to take in violence but not retaliate, come what may. Women set up a makeshift medical unit, prepared for any violence on the part of the British.

Four hundred policemen, commanded by six British officers, were present on the scene. The volunteers slowly marched forward in columns and Webb Miller, an American journalist, was on hand to witness this event; he describes it in vivid detail:

> *Suddenly at a word of command, scores of*
> *...policemen rushed upon the advancing marchers*
> *and rained blows on their heads with their steel shod*
> *lathas [batons]. Not one of the marchers even raised*
> *an arm to fend off the blows. They went down like*
> *ninepins. From where I stood, I heard the sickening*
> *whack of the clubs on unprotected skulls.... Those*
> *struck down fell sprawling unconscious or writhing*
> *with fractured skulls or broken shoulders.... Although*
> *everyone knew that within a few minutes he would be*
> *beaten down, perhaps killed, I could detect no signs*
> *of wavering or fear....They [the volunteers] marched*
> *steadily, with heads up... The police commenced to*
> *savagely kick the seated men in the abdomen and*
> *testicles and then dragged them by their arms and*
> *feet and threw them in the ditches.... Hour after hour*
> *stretcher-bearers carried back a stream of inert*
> *bleeding bodies.³*

Thus the volunteers marched, column after column, neither cringing nor retreating. At the end of it, 320 men lay injured and two had died, but not a single blow had been retaliated to.

It was the reporting of these and many other events that showed the immoral stranglehold of Britain that could no longer be justified. It showed Britain as a heartless and greedy exploiter of areas outside its own borders. Independence for India now seemed inevitable — it would soon become a surety, and the question would only be when and in what shape would that freedom come to India. In the year 1946, Britain announced that they would be leaving India. India had won her freedom, but dark times loomed ahead.

The Calcutta Fast

The year was now 1947, and India was on the verge of independence. But freedom would come not to one nation, but two: India was to be divided and a separate nation for Muslims called Pakistan would be formed. Gandhi had vehemently opposed this. He could not bear to see the partition of his beloved India, and he had always nurtured and nourished the hope that Hindus and Muslims could live together in harmony. But Hindu-Muslim riots were becoming a regular feature, and with partition imminent, what was always an uneasy truce between the two was now marked by open and violent hostility. Cases of arson, looting and murder were increasing, and all of this culminated in a vicious bloodbath that came to be known as the "Great Calcutta Killing." In a mere four days, 4,000 people died and another 11,000 were injured in a tremendous orgy of violence and hatred — the degree of which had hitherto been unseen. People saw that the spiral of violence was now escalating and spreading dramatically across the rest of the country. It seemed like India was on the verge of civil war.

British resources were spread thin after the Second World War. The army and police were all woefully inadequate. The local state government, driven by party and religious loyalties and administrators lacking in experience, threw up their hands in despair. India was rapidly descending into chaos. Gandhi was going through the darkest period of his life: his method of Satyagraha was looking largely like a failure, for although he had all his life preached and practiced non-violence, now his people were tearing each other apart.

Gandhi had long ago withdrawn from politics on a national level. He had been quietly working in small villages, attempting to uplift them and remove the blot of untouchability, and bring about self-sufficiency. He was 77 years old and had become a famous man, revered at home and tremendously respected abroad. He had bequeathed to the world a new way of fighting for peace that used truth and love as powerful weapons. He had demonstrated that nonviolence; compassion and truth were not mere sentimental, sappy words or ideals that were "out of touch" with the real world, but rather powerful, palpable forces that were remarkably effective. But in August 1947, when India was celebrating her independence, Gandhi was not a happy man. He was in his ashram, observing a day of fasting and quiet. His mind was on the violence that was unfolding across the country. Finding very little reason for celebrating, he asked, *would it not be more appropriate to send condolences?*

Large parts of India were sliding into anarchy, and hate was threatening to engulf the nation. Gandhi would rise to the occasion — and magnificently so, albeit for the last time. The killings and violence around the country was continuing unabated. Gandhi arrived in Calcutta, where the violence was at its worst. Gandhi, unprotected, moved through riot- afflicted localities, and even took up residence amidst Muslim friends as a symbol of unity. He toured the riot-torn areas, and held prayer meetings where men and women — victims from both communities — turned out in large numbers to share their grievances. He told the crowd that his "head hung in shame at this recital of man's barbarism."

Gandhi became a "shoulder to cry on" for the men and women who had lost their loved ones. Slowly, Gandhi's presence began to bring about a calm, and within nine days, remarkably, a city torn by violence for so long was returning to normalcy. It would not be long, however, before violence would erupt again. Gandhi, who had seemingly exhausted all his resources, now resorted to his one last "infallible weapon." He announced that he would fast, and would not stop until complete peace, calm and sanity had returned to the city.

All the people around him dissuaded him. Gandhi was more than 77 years old now, and they felt that he would not be able to take the severe stress it placed on his body. Although he had fasted in the past for Hindu-Muslim unity and for the removal of untouchability and had been successful, many doubted if this fast would have any positive effect on the city. In fact, on the first day of the fast, there was no change whatsoever, and the violence and riots persisted.

On the second day, however, peace and calm slowly returned. As the news of Gandhi's fasting and the deterioration of his health spread around the city, Calcutta would witness its most dramatic turnaround. A large mixed procession of Hindus and Muslims came and promised to reconcile their differences. Then peace demonstrations, with both communities involved, began to parade around the city. On the third day, gangs that had taken part in the violence showed up and admitted their complicity while surrendering their weapons and arms. By the end of the third day, all violence had ceased. Gandhi had once again prevailed.

Crowds began to throng Gandhi's residence and were pleading with him to stop the fast. Finally, after asking for and receiving a written pledge from all politicians, administrators and party leaders that they would do their utmost to ensure non-violence and peace, Gandhi broke his fast to the relief and joy of the crowd. It came to be known as the "Calcutta miracle"; one historian called it Gandhi's "finest hour," and British historian E W.R. Lumby wrote many years later on that fast that

> *His triumph was complete, and the peace that he brought was destined to endure.... He had in fact worked a miracle, perhaps the greatest of modern times.*[4]

Gandhi's appeal to the conscience had once again worked. But his work was far from done. With the rest of India still under a shroud of violence, Gandhi, 77 years old, embarked on a "village-a-day pilgrimage." He walked through some of the worst-affected areas, a walking tour of 116 miles that covered 47 villages. Village by village, he worked his wonders. Miscreants had thrown shattered glass on the streets, but Gandhi was not easily perturbed. As biographer Judith Brown writes,

> *...He went into the eye of the storm, into places where violence was most terrifying; he became the sole satyagrahi [upholder of truth], a man who pitted himself totally against violence by personal demonstration as well as preaching and fasting...*[5]

People once again flocked to share with him their grievances. He was like an expert therapist, listening patiently to the grievances of the victims, holding prayer meetings, and exhorting them to uphold the higher standards of tolerance and love. Nicholas Mansergh, a renowned historian, writes that

> *In this, the last year of his life, Gandhi's influence was transcendent.... It was his preaching of the doctrine of non-violence more than any other single factor that stood between India and bloodshed on a frightful scale.*[6]

As Buddha had said, "Hate does not cease by hate, by love alone it ceases. This is eternal law". Gandhi was proof of that law. The "Calcutta miracle" and the "village-a-day pilgrimage" would prove to be the last of his campaigns. On January 30, 1948, Gandhi was shot dead by a fanatic belonging to a Hindu extremist group.

20

More than Body and Mind

According to the mystics, most of us, most of the time, are aware of only a very small part of our own being. We rarely dive below the waters of our surface life. This is why in every religious and metaphysical tradition, there is some remark regarding most of mankind as "sleep walking" or being "half asleep": being aware of only a very miniscule part of ourselves, we assume this part to be the whole of us. As India's philosopher sage Sri Aurobindo puts it, what we see "on the surface is a small and diminished representation of our secret greater existence."[1]

Gandhi intuited what many philosophers and the wisdom traditions of the past have alluded to: that human beings are more than a body with a brain. There is more to us than what meets the eye. We are a body and a mind, but with a soul or spirit. While we all have a body and inhabit a physical realm that is subject to the laws of space and time, we are also spiritual beings. According to the great mystics, saints and sages, deep within us is a *centre of transcendent awareness* that has been variously called "atman" in Hinduism, "Buddha nature" in Buddhism, the "higher self," soul, and so forth. This "deep within" is the source of our compassion and unconditional love, and it is what drives us to seek truth, beauty and justice. Gandhi was deeply convinced of this; he did not accept this on blind faith, but instead tested and validated this in his own life by engaging in regular spiritual practice.

The modern scientific worldview acknowledges only the body, and partially the mind. The unfortunate consequence of such a limited view is that there are large parts of us that lay unknown to us and hence unused by us. However, we can see from the lives of great men and women that to live fully, creatively, passionately and wholeheartedly means to use and engage all of our muscles: the physical, mental, emotional and spiritual. To neglect our spiritual side is to have an incomplete view of ourselves and reality. In the process, we sell ourselves short, because such as view is partial, reductionist and one-dimensional, and our deeper parts are confined to a peripheral status.

There is a very great difference in how the western scientific community (predominantly) views the human body as compared to the eastern wisdom traditions. The eastern wisdom traditions explicitly state that the body is not made up of inert clumps of matter (as we are conditioned to think) but rather our bodies are a flow of energy and information that is connected to the universal intelligence, or the cosmic mind. The eastern viewpoint is that mind and body are not separate, but are rather inseparably intertwined and connected.

In fact, modern medicine is waking up to the fact that there may be more to the mind than has been previously acknowledged. An increasing number of people are now trying alternative and complementary heath care approaches that are based on a holistic rather than materialistic view of the human body. Recognising this shift, almost all the prestigious medical schools now offer to their students courses on alternative and complementary medicine. What was earlier considered radical and even "weird" or "quack" ideas are now being investigated and researched by some of the most prominent institutions and researchers. There is a great deal of research being carried out, for example, on the healing effects of prayer, meditation, yoga, chanting, music, tai chi, massage and visualisation.

The most effective therapies, it has been noted, are the ones that deal with more than just the body, and also address the mind. It is not uncommon these days to see cancer patients complement and supplement chemotherapy with other approaches like psychotherapy, group support, counselling and journaling, prayer, meditation, contemplation, yoga, tai chi and so forth. These approaches attend to the *whole* person (i.e., not only to their physical bodies, but also to their psychological, emotional, spiritual and cultural dimensions).

We sometimes mistakenly assume that there is only one way to know the world, and that is through science. Science alone, however, does not have the language or the methodology to quench the deeper yearning of the soul. When we turn to scientists, we can know about the physical laws of the universe, chemical compositions, and the material aspects of our world. We are told of super strings, atoms, molecules, huge distances between planets, mathematical formulae, numbers, quantities and the like. This is no doubt quite interesting, fascinating and extremely valuable. But when we want to know the spiritual qualities of the cosmos, then we turn to the mystic, saint, sage, prophet or poet. *Is the universe compassionate, benevolent or hostile? Is there a purpose or meaning to life? What is love? What is death?* These are questions that cannot be adequately answered by science alone. We have to turn to spirituality for these answers. That is why every culture has had myths, religion, folklore, fairy tales, poetry, philosophy, arts, music, paintings and so forth: they all speak the language of the heart and soul. All of these disciplines have something very valuable to teach us about life, and how to live it. All of them help us better understand the world and our relationship to it. Our world, the cosmos, life and the universe are infinitely richer than what science alone can describe.

The modern west has assumed that there is only one way — or a vastly superior way — to reality, and that is the scientific, rational, empirical way. Today we see an over- dependence on the scientific, logical, theoretical, abstract, mathematical and conceptual modes of knowing. Authentic self-knowledge is not possible merely through sense, reason, ideas or conceptual knowledge alone. In order to know one's innermost self and in order to tap into our spiritual selves, we must use other instruments such as contemplation, intuition, meditation and prayer. These techniques and practices are all part of genuine spiritual disciplines that have been developed, honed and used by the world's greatest mystical and wisdom traditions over thousands of years, with their main objective being to help people experience the deepest truth for themselves.

The head denotes reason and logic, while the heart symbolises intuition. We are all simultaneously scientists and artists, although modem society holds reason and logic in high esteem while often neglecting intuition. We assume that through logic and reason everything can be known and measured — but, as Dennis Burkitt wrote, *not everything that counts can be counted.* Great people such as Gandhi have the ideal combination of heart and head, of reason and intuition. We must pay homage to and listen to both the artist and the scientist within us, because from them both we can learn much.

21

The Importance of Trust

It is the nature of man to rise to greatness if greatness is expected of him.

- John Steinbeck (1902-1968)

As we grow up, we all tend to acquire an implicit understanding of the world and our place in it. We hold a set of assumptions — largely hidden from our conscious awareness — about the essential nature of the world. These core beliefs and assumptions, although hidden, wield a tremendous influence on our everyday behaviour. Albert Einstein was once asked by a friend, "What is the most important question?" To which Einstein replied, "Is the universe friendly?" Einstein was no psychologist, but he had unearthed, quite intuitively, the heart of the matter. Our view of the world as being either benevolent or hostile deeply impacts and shapes our thoughts, attitudes and actions.

There is one worldview that insists that the world is a hostile place. It portrays the nature of human beings as essentially selfish, narrowly individualistic and aggressive. The social landscape is seen as a battleground where power and aggression is required to get ahead. People who hold such a view like to invoke metaphors and terms such as "survival of the fittest," "the law of the jungle," "killer instinct," and so forth. In this view, life is seen as an everyday fight for survival. Human beings are said to be looking out only for their own interests, and will cooperate only if it means personal advancement.

Gandhi did not buy into this view. In fact, he believed in quite the opposite: he believed that, at its heart, the universe was benevolent, and that human beings were fundamentally good. But Gandhi was not naïve. He was well aware of the evils perpetrated by human beings on their fellow men and women. Gandhi lived through two world wars. It was an era when every day brought news of cruelty and misery from some part of the world. Moreover, he struggled with his own shortcomings; he was painfully aware of the petty jealousies, greed and anger within himself. He was conscious of the levels to which human beings could stoop, but was simultaneously aware of the heights to which a human being could rise. He was aware of what the "better angels of our nature" were capable of.

Thus, well aware of the great viciousness and cruelty of which mankind was individually and collectively capable, he held a firm and abiding trust that one could rise above it. He believed that human beings hold the capacity and the urge to transcend their greed, anger, jealousy and egoistic pride. Not only could human beings rise above their pettiness, they *wanted* to rise above it. Nelson Mandela said it best: *Man's goodness is a flame that can be hidden but never extinguished.* Gandhi had a deeply abiding trust in that goodness, and his methods were suited for speaking to that goodness within human beings.

In Gandhi's worldview, no matter how cruel a person seemed, an appeal could always be made to the person's higher instincts — that person's "better self." An "implicit trust in human nature" was the very essence of his creed, and this is why Gandhi refused to use any manipulative, deceptive or violent techniques or strategies against the British, despite the cause of freedom being noble and just. For Gandhi, the ends never justified the means.

The trust that Gandhi placed on humankind in general and on his followers in particular had a self-fulfilling tendency. By behaving as if people were capable of much more than they believed themselves to be capable of, Gandhi pulled them towards a higher standard of conduct. Gandhi expected the best from his followers, and they rose to those expectations. As the American novelist John Steinbeck said, *It is the nature of man to rise to greatness if greatness is expected of him.* Gandhi saw higher possibilities and potentialities in human beings; people responded to it and were able to tap into their higher capacities. By placing this implicit trust in their abilities, he empowered his followers.

This phenomenon has actually been proved through research. Back in 1968, a well-known psychologist by the name of Robert Rosenthal conducted a fascinating experiment.[1] Rosenthal, along with his fellow researcher, randomly divided a class of students into two groups. They then told teachers that one group had been identified as "intellectual bloomers," and that they held considerably greater potential than the other group. (In reality, there was no difference between the two groups; the students had been arbitrarily chosen.) However, at the end of the year, the students who had been labelled as "intelligent" actually showed a marked level of improvement in their performance. In short: the grades and performances of the students merely labelled as "high achievers" actually went up!

The researchers explained the phenomena thus: when the teachers were told that these students were clever, the teacher's expectations were raised. The teachers actually spent more quality time with these students and gave them extra attention. The students, receiving this extra care and quality time, felt nurtured; this enhanced both their confidence and their sense of self worth, and enabled them to improve upon their performance. The students lived up to their label of being "intelligent". The teacher's heightened belief and raised expectations in the ability of the children raised the children's performance levels.

Since this landmark study was done, this phenomenon — called the "Pygmalion effect" — has been confirmed and documented in a number of other research studies. It proves that people respond to the level of confidence and expectations that you place upon them. Our belief in people often becomes a reality, and Gandhi created better behaviour in people by both believing in them and expecting better behaviour of them. They became more fully engaged and motivated, and thus tapped fully into their capabilities. His positive expectations of human nature actually created that reality.

22

The Law of Personal Responsibility

People are always blaming their circumstances for what they are. I don't believe in circumstances. The people who get on in this world are the people who get up and look for the circumstances they want, and, if they can't find them, make them.

- George Bernard Shaw (1856–1950)

One of the hallmarks of the fully integrated, self-aware human being is the ability to take personal responsibility for the actions and choices. Such people hold themselves personally accountable for their lives. If some aspect of their lives is not going well, rather than blaming their genes, parents, cultural conditioning or God, they pro-actively set out to change that aspect of their lives. Taking responsibility for one's own life is the essential *sine-qua-non* for success and happiness: it is the most basic requirement, and the bare minimum that is required. None of our dreams will come true in our lives until we take responsibility and make things happen.

We are responsible in large measure for many of the things that happen to us. The quality of our lives, the quality of our relationships, the jobs we find ourselves in, our body weight — all are almost entirely of our own making. If we want to significantly and positively impact our futures through our actions, then we will first have to honestly admit to ourselves that we have played an active role in creating our lives up to this point in time. Our past actions and choices, taken consciously or unconsciously, have determined our present situation in life. By thus taking responsibility for our lives, we move from a victim mentality to a co-creator mentality. We take conscious control of our future and put ourselves in charge.

The eastern wisdom traditions of Hinduism and Buddhism speak of the Law of Karma. This is known more simply as the law of cause-and-effect. Karma literally means "action" or "doing," and this law basically implies that we are responsible for the consequences of our actions. It teaches that every action is inevitably accompanied by its due effect, and that when we choose an action, we invariably choose a consequence. Because cause and effect are inseparable, what we are today is the direct result of our past actions and thoughts — and what we will be tomorrow is dependent upon our present choices and actions. This may be a very daunting thought, but we all have some intuitive understanding of this law when we say, "we reap what we sow" or "what goes around, comes around." We tend to use these sayings only in the negative sense, but it works in the positive sense as well.

Whether one believes in the eastern philosophies of reincarnation and rebirth or not, the Law of Karma teaches that every day, through our choices and actions, we weave the fabric of our future destiny. What we will be in the future is dependent upon the choices we make today, and if we choose wisely, then we will enjoy the positive consequences of that choice. To state it in a very simple, if not obvious way: if we want apples, we must sow apple seeds. We cannot sow orange seeds and expect apples. The right speech, right thinking and right actions will have the right consequences, and they will improve not only our own happiness but also affect the happiness of those around us. As Swami Vivekananda has said, *Karma is the eternal assertion of human freedom.... Our thoughts, our words and deeds are the threads of the net which we throw around ourselves.*

Many people wrongly assume that Karma is fatalism, determinism or predestination. They think that Karma is a matter of fate, to which we must helplessly submit. If this were true and the course of our lives were completely determined, then free will — our ability to choose — would be nothing more than a fiction. If our lives are indeed completely predestined, then our fates are sealed independent of any action on our part. But the Law of Karma teaches otherwise; it places responsibility for our happiness squarely on our own shoulders. It states that we are the architects of our own fate. As the Buddha stated, *we are the heirs of our own actions.* When one understands this correctly, it is both freeing and empowering. Beyond instincts, beyond social conditioning and beyond childhood programming, we are free to choose the paths that our lives take. We have the freedom to think thoughts, make decisions and take actions that will help rather than hinder us.

How far does this personal responsibility go? There are, without a doubt, many events in our lives — some more seminal than others — over which we had no control. For instance, we did not have a say regarding what sort of parents or siblings we got. We had no choice in deciding whether we were born into a rich or a poor family. We had no say in the kind of genes we were endowed with. We had no choice regarding the kind of social conditioning we were exposed to as a child. There is no doubt that all these events do significantly affect the trajectories of our lives. These may be "random" events, but our reactions to these "chance" events are still very much under our control. As Epictetus proposed 2,000 years ago: *people are not disturbed by the events that happen to them, but by their view of what happens to them.* More importantly, how we choose to react to a particular event will determine the outcome of the succeeding event, because *our reactions change what ensues.* For example, sales people who do not let their hopes and optimism be affected by consistent rejections turn out to be very successful in the long run. In direct contrast, sales people who react negatively to rejection by saying to themselves, "I am no good" or "Nobody wants to buy anything from me" will give up much more quickly, and are likely to quit the job altogether.[1]

We can illustrate this phenomenon better with our fictional example of John (whom we first met in another chapter on choosing between fear and growth). As you will remember, John started psychotherapy in order to deal with the problems he had in his marriage. John had a very unhappy childhood; his father abandoned him at the age of seven, and his mother had been an alcoholic. John did not choose those events, nor did he have a say in selecting his parents. But John had the power within himself to take responsibility for how he would react to those childhood events as an adult. He was, as a child, undoubtedly a victim of circumstances, incidents and events beyond his control. As a grown up, however, he had the personal freedom to choose how he would let those events affect his life. As we saw in that example, after many trials and tribulations, John did exercise his personal freedom and responsibility, and broke out of his victim mentality.

Even within the realm of spirituality, the importance of personal action — of taking responsibility for one's own growth — is central. Self-effort is essential if we want freedom from fear and insecurity, and want to awaken to our higher self. As the Indian saint Sri Ramakrishna remarked, *the winds of grace are always blowing, but we must raise our sails to catch it.*

As mentioned earlier in this book, although the issue of free will and fate has been debated endlessly since the very dawn of civilisation, it has never been completely and satisfactorily resolved. But it is a self-fulfilling prophecy that has the capacity to affect the quality of our lives. When one goes through life blaming circumstances, events, conditions and other people for one's present conditions, it puts us in "victim mode." We begin to make excuses for the state of our lives and, more often than not, become resigned to our fate. The only way in which we can transcend these limitations, genetic programming and cultural conditioning is to accept that the choice to rise above these circumstances still lies with us. Until we accept responsibility for our lives, we will remain a product of our past and our genetic and social conditioning.

Gandhi believed in taking personal responsibility. He did not see responsibility as a burden, but rather as a great source of personal power. He saw it as a powerful tool that human beings possessed to fashion changes in their lives. According to Gandhi, at any given point in time people can take responsibility for their lives and begin to make changes and improvements in accordance with their own deeply-held values and principles. Whatever our present condition, we can choose — however limited our choices may be — and slowly increase our personal freedom.

One can begin this process right away, without waiting for others to share these convictions. When one adopts the changes in one's own life, then inevitably other people will begin to emulate that change when they see the positive effects of doing so. In fact, this theme is central to Gandhi's life and his message. In his words, "we must become the change we wish to see in the world." This was one of Gandhi's core tenets, and it was one of his deep beliefs and convictions. In his opinion, the actions and choices of one individual had far-reaching and potentially wide consequences. Ultimately the fate of the nation depended on the personal responsibility displayed by each one of its members. One could lay the foundation for a true moral community by working on oneself. When one thus initiates a change within oneself, he or she would have a ripple effect that would slowly but surely begin to affect their environment. As Gandhi wrote,

> *The world of tomorrow will be, must be, a society based on non-violence....It may seem a distant goal, an impractical Utopia. But it is not in the least unobtainable, since it can be worked from the here and now. An individual can adopt...the non-violent way-without having to wait for others to do so. And if an individual can do it, cannot whole groups of individuals? Whole nations?[1]*

One individual could thus make a huge difference. In his own lifetime, Gandhi himself was breathing proof and the living embodiment of this principle. We have seen what can happen when one committed individual makes an initiative for change. But this change must begin with us. It all starts with our ability to think in the right manner, because action is the physical expression of thought. When we understand that we become that which we think, we can deliberately sow good thoughts, attitudes and actions. Slowly but surely, due to the Law of Karma, we will reap the benefits of these initiatives. As Buddha put it,

> *The thought manifests as the word;*
> *The word manifests as the deed;*
> *The deed develops into habit;*
> *And habit hardens into character;*

So watch the thought and its ways with care,
And let it spring from love
Born out of concern for all beings....
As the shadow follows the body,
As we think, so we become.

23

A Sense of Mystery and Miracle

Explore everything around you, penetrate to the furthest limits of human knowledge, and always you will come up with something inexplicable in the end. It is called life.

- Albert Schweitzer (1875-1965)

One of the core foundations of wisdom is the understanding that there is an inexplicable, inherent mystery to the nature of things. Some of the greatest saints, sages and mystics have lived in a state of awareness where they perceived all of life — *everything* — as a mystery and a miracle. The feeling that life is a mysterious and miraculous force pervaded their lives. Walt Whitman, the American poet wrote, *as to me, I know of nothing else but miracles.* We inhabit a profoundly mysterious universe. Many of the things that we most take for granted are often the most mysterious and miraculous. For these men and women a sunrise, a sunset, the sight of a newborn, the blooming of a flower, the changing of seasons, the flight of a bird, the smile of a child — these are all profoundly and inexplicably miraculous. They stand in awe and wonder at the beauty and mystery of this world. No less a figure than Albert Einstein wrote,

The most beautiful thing we can experience is the mysterious. It is the source of all true art and all science. He to whom this emotion is a stranger, who can no longer pause to wonder and stand rapt in awe, is as good as dead: his eyes are closed.

No matter how much we know about this universe and its origins, there is something inherently miraculous about it. No matter how much scientific data we gather, there is still a mystery at the heart of things. We have theories, facts, labels, explanations and concepts, yet behind it all there is something utterly inexplicable, profound and enigmatic. Take the case of "love": we have all felt it, we all yearn for it, and we can sense when it is present. We "know" what it is and yet ultimately, at its core, it is a phenomenon that is still very mysterious. Love is too deep, too vast and too profound to be limited or fitted within the framework of words, concepts and theories. Poets, philosophers and even scientists have written reams and reams of pages on this topic, and yet it remains an enigma, utterly indefinable. The distinguished psychologist Carl Jung wrote in his famous book *Memories, Dreams, Reflections:*

> *Man can try to name love, showering upon it all the names at his command, and still he will involve himself in endless self-deceptions. If he possesses a grain of wisdom, he will lay down his arms and name the unknown by the more unknown — that is, by the name of God.*[1]

We have all had moments in our lives that were deeply moving and profoundly emotional — for example, the first time when we fell in love or when we first held a newborn in our hands or when we witnessed a sunset from the seashore. In such moments, we may have felt a profound sense of interconnectedness and belonging, however fleeting; something inside of us shifts, and perhaps we glimpse a more sacred reality. In such moments, there is often the feeling within us that we could not quite put into words, but yet we could sense a deeper mystery.

Throughout the ages, saints, sages and holy men and women have always understood that this mystery defies full understanding by our rational modes of thought. They are well aware that this reality cannot be quite captured with words and language. It can be sensed, intuited, felt, and maybe even expressed through a poem, painting or sculpture — but it is ultimately beyond language. Yet, in our modern era, we feel that anything can be explained and put into words. Paradoxically, poets who "have a way with words" understand the limits of language better than anybody else. As Rainer Maria Rilke, the celebrated German poet writes in *Letters to a Young Poet,*

> *Things are not all so tangible and expressible as others would typically have us believe; most experiences are indefinable for they happen in a realm where no word has ever entered...*

Most of us, however, are intolerant of ambiguity and mystery. We demand black and white guidelines, rules, and clear-cut formulae. We also tend to take the beauty and mystery around us for granted, and oftentimes we are too busy proving our knowledge or showing off our cleverness. A comfortable set of labels, theories and words take on the guise of "explanation," essentially blinding us to the deeper miracles of life. The Sufi mystic and poet extraordinaire Rumi advises us thus:

> *Sell your cleverness and buy bewilderment;*
> *Cleverness is mere opinion,*
> *Bewilderment is intuition.*

People like Gandhi, Thoreau and Emerson have all had this sense of the mysterious, or the miraculous. Their words and descriptions were couched in their respective cultural contexts and their times, but they all alluded to a greater mystery. They sensed the presence of a greater power that both includes and transcends our material reality. They felt that there are more dimensions to our lives (and to us) than we usually comprehend. This spiritual feeling is at the very centres and cores of their lives. Here is how Gandhi described his feeling of the mysterious and miraculous:

> *There is an indefinable mysterious Power that pervades everything. I feel it, though I do not see it. It is this unseen Power, which makes itself felt and yet defies all proof, because it is so unlike all that I perceive through my senses. It transcends the senses.*[2]

Religion, in its truest sense, attempts to comprehend this mystery. It evokes a sense of oneness with life, and a sense of harmonious interconnectedness that results in a deep reverence and sanctity for all life. Religion and spirituality have a component of awe, wonder and amazement, but for many "religious" and "pious" people, religion is little more than a set of practices, rituals, beliefs and doctrines. The outer religion is followed, but this inward religious experience (of mystery) seems to be profoundly lacking. As Carl Jung remarked, for many *religious people, religion stands in the way of the religious experience.*

Life and its problems take on a depressing tone when we become blind to this sense of mystery. When we let the hustle and bustle of everyday, mundane existence take priority, we will invariably lose sight of this mystery. Abraham Maslow, the pioneering psychologist who studied the characteristics of self-actualising people, found that all highly creative and self-fulfilled people possess the ability to be to be awed and fascinated by things that others often take for granted.[3]

It is no accident that all those who feel this sense of mystery undergo a profound shift of consciousness. More often than not, these very same individuals also possess abundant compassion, radiate a loving kindness and have a sense that all beings are sacred. They find meaning not only in their own lives, but find the entire universe — all of life and the very cosmos — suffused with benevolent meaning and purpose. A deep sense of gratitude becomes apparent in their behaviour — a sense of gratitude for being able to experience the miracle called life. To them, even the seemingly mundane appears miraculous. They no longer search for miracles, for life *is the* miracle.

24

The Power of ideals

An ideal has an indispensable value for practice, in that thought thereby gives to action its right aim.[1]

- Plato

We all hold ideals, lofty goals, mighty dreams and yearnings. However, many of us hesitate to undertake a task unless we feel we can completely achieve it; we seem to want a guarantee that it can be fully achieved. We feel that the task is not worth undertaking unless it is completely realisable, to its full perfection. But Gandhi knew otherwise, and he knew that such an attitude is a stumbling block to our growth. As Gandhi wrote,

Men generally hesitate to make a beginning, if they feel that the objective cannot be had in its entirety. Such an attitude of mind is in reality a bar to progress.[2]

Consider the following statements: "Since I can never be completely truthful, I will quit trying to be truthful"; "Since there can never be complete peace and harmony in the world, I will stop working for peace"; "Since greed and acquisitiveness can never be completely removed from the human heart, it is futile to even try." We can see the absurdity of these statements. Whether they are fully achieved or not, we would all acknowledge that these are worthy and noble goals.

Let us look at Gandhi's ideal. His vision had two specific components: one was to achieve freedom for India through non-violence; the second, larger ideal was for all of humanity to grow and evolve toward a world of peace and harmony. Many ridiculed Gandhi when he spoke of his vision for the whole of humanity. They suggested that it was a fool's dream to expect people to live in complete harmony and peace the world over. But Gandhi gave the following answer to his critics.

> *I may be taunted with the retort that this is all Utopian and, therefore, not worth a single thought.... [Nevertheless] let India live for this true picture [of peace and harmony], though never realisable in its completeness. We must have a picture of what we want, before we can have something approaching it.*[3]

Even though our ideals and our conceptions of a perfect world may never be completely realisable, they still hold great practical value in giving our life direction. Gandhi strongly rejected the notion that an experiment or an ideal is worthwhile only if it can be fully achieved. Even if it is never fully achieved in its entirety, it is still invaluable because in a world without ideals, mankind would be doomed to mediocrity. The attitude of "why bother with something that can never be achieved" is to give into the forces of entropy, and leads to atrophy in our capacities and faculties. Gandhi felt that ideals are indispensable for human beings, because it gives one a direction and a goal to work towards.

Gandhi emphasised that when we attempt to live our life *as if* the ideal could be fully achieved, much can be accomplished. His own life bears witness to this. Since his death in 1948, his teachings and his methods have inspired and influenced many liberation movements around the world — most notably, the civil rights struggle in America, spearheaded by Martin Luther King, Jr.; the South African struggle, headed by Nelson Mandela; and the Polish solidarity movement, led by Lech Walesa. Gandhi's ideas and philosophies have also influenced pioneers from disciplines as diverse as economics, spirituality, conflict resolution, politics and ecology. By living his life *as if* his ideals could be achieved, Gandhi left behind a rich and lasting legacy for the world.

25

<u>Personal Honesty and Authenticity</u>

*To thine own self be true, and it follows as the night
the day, thou canst not be false to any man.*

-William Shakespeare (1564-1616)

Gandhi had an unwavering commitment to the values of
integrity, transparency and honesty. He made a conscious
choice to live his life guided by these values. He was
constantly on the lookout for any traces of deception
within him, so that he could root them out. He strived to
become *authentic,* which is the ability to be oneself in front
of others. Gandhi did not wear any masks — he always
displayed his real self. He was not afraid of letting others
know who he really was. With Gandhi, what you saw was
what you got, and that was why he engendered such a
tremendous amount of trust and goodwill, even from many
of his opponents.

We all indulge in pretence and playacting, to a greater or
lesser extent. In our corporate and social lives, we maintain
a façade. We act in one way, on the surface, when we are
experiencing something else underneath. We act as though
we know the answers when we clearly don't. We pretend
that we are self-assured when we are actually feeling
frightened and unsure. A life filled with such pretence is
like a slow poisoning of our true selves, because there is
always an inner urge within each one of us — a yearning —
for greater transparency and authenticity. Neglecting that
urge often has a debilitating effect on our physical, mental

and emotional well-being. As Boris Pasternak wrote in *Doctor Zhivago*,

> *The great majority of us are required to live a life of constant systematic duplicity. Your health is bound to be affected if day after day, you say the opposite of what you feel, if you grovel before what you dislike and rejoice at what brings you nothing but misfortune. Our nervous system isn't just a fiction; it's a part of our physical body, and our soul exists in space and is inside us, like the teeth in our mouth. It cannot be forever violated with impunity.*

Our ability to be truthful with others is possible only when we attempt to be transparent and truthful with ourselves. The truthful person engages in consistent, unvarying truth-telling with him or herself.

However, we are all prone to self-deception; it manifests itself in our day-to-day behaviour, through denials, rationalisations, cover-ups, justifications, excuses, finger-pointing and evasions of responsibility. We are very eager to point out the faults of others, but remain blind to our own faults and errors. We are our own public relations experts, in that we often edit and change reality to make it more palatable to ourselves. We tell ourselves stories, even as the facts stare us in the face. We are constantly putting our own spin on reality.

Telling the truth to others requires us to first develop the ability to see reality as it is, without distorting it or being defensive about it. Self-awareness is a prerequisite, a necessary precondition, for honesty with oneself; it is only through a growing self-awareness that we are able to see how our own distortions and defence mechanisms become obstacles in our path towards authenticity, growth and maturity.

Philosophers and sages tell us that as human beings, we have an internal *urge towards honesty* and authenticity. That is why we admire people who are honest. Research shows that the number one quality we most look for in our leaders is honesty and integrity.[1] Moreover, we all intuitively seek environments and people with whom we can be ourselves, and accepted for who we are. We all crave intimacy, where we can drop our defences. Something within us abhors and grows tired of being "in costume" all the time. Our inner being seeks an authentic engagement with life, and Gandhi got in touch with this urge within himself. He attempted his very best to make his life "an open book" — to himself, and to others.

True to this form, in his autobiography, Gandhi held nothing back. By the time he began writing his memoirs, Gandhi was already perceived as the "Mahatma," or "great soul," and was widely accepted as a spiritual and moral leader. In his autobiography, however, Gandhi did not cover up the facts, attempt to portray himself in a favourable light, or protect his image as the "Mahatma who could do no wrong." On the contrary, he was brutally honest. He highlighted all his perceived errors and faults. He wrote candidly of his shortcomings, his struggles, his mistakes and his "Himalayan blunders." He did not worry that admitting to such mistakes, errors and faults would damage his reputation or his image as a spiritual or political leader.

Gandhi attempted always to speak the truth as best he could, without the intention to mislead, trick or deceive. He did not resort to cheating, lying or subterfuge, even with his opponents. Just before undertaking any major event such as a strike or a march, he would write to the British viceroys and other authorities, fully disclosing his plans. Whatever he said or did, he did so in full view. He felt that there was no need to hide or do things in a clandestine manner, because he believed that he was fighting for a just cause. As he put it, "Truth never damages a cause that is just."

Gandhi learned at a very young age the power of honesty. Around the time he was 15, Gandhi stole a bit of gold from his house to help out a friend. No sooner was the deed done, he was visited by a terrible sense of guilt. After much agonising of conscience, he vowed never to steal again. Feeling a deep urge to come clean about his crime but lacking the courage to speak, he wrote out a confession to his father. He asked for the penalty that was due for the crime, pledged never to steal again; he also pleaded with his father not to punish himself for the sins of his child. The father was on his sick bed when Gandhi, trembling in fear, handed him the letter. Upon reading the confession, the father was so deeply moved that tears began streaming down his cheeks. Too weak to speak, the father simply tore up the letter. Gandhi wept with joy. Years later, he would write that this was to him an abject lesson in the transformative power of "Ahimsa" (the love born out of truth and non-violence), and he wrote in his autobiography that *those pearl drops of love cleansed my heart and washed my sins away.*[2]

Where truth, honesty and transparency were concerned, Gandhi did not engage in politics of expediency. He would not manipulate the truth according to the circumstances. He did not resort to the "whatever works" model of living, because he knew that this is a slippery slope that erodes one's values and brings down one's standards. We may gain in the short term, but we pay a serious price in the long run. He did not use the circumstances to justify his behaviour, but instead attempted to be as honest as could be in all situations. Gandhi also avoided rationalisations or excuses for not telling the truth. (Whenever we resort to lying or subtle deception, we tend to use excuses such as "everybody does it," "this is the real world" or "we have to be practical")

Today, we are suffering from a crisis of truth. Surveys indicate that many high school students do not see anything wrong with cheating or lying. Many of them feel that in today's world, if one wants to get ahead and become someone special, then cheating is necessary and unavoidable. In a world of exaggerated ad campaigns, profit-at-all-costs companies and political spin-doctors, truth-telling and honesty is becoming rather difficult to find. Doing the right thing demands more effort and vigilance then ever before.

For Gandhi, honesty and truthfulness was not a tactic or a superficial technique to win favours or to portray a good social image. It was a fundamental component of his ethical character, as well as the ultimate goal of his spiritual and moral quest. Having the right speech was a central concern and preoccupation for Gandhi because, for him, truth was God. He believed deeply in the statement made by the ancient seers and sages of India: "Satyam Eva Jayate," which means "Truth Alone Triumphs."

The Learning Orientation

The art of living is intricately connected to learning. How well we live is directly dependent upon how well we learn from life. We are- all born learners: one look at young children will show us that curiosity and the love of learning is innate. In children we see this natural, innate curiosity to learn and know their world. Although we are born learners, in our later years, the protection of our self-esteem and social image seems to take precedence. Moreover, we become socially conditioned and see learning as synonymous with grades, rankings and awards (including scholarships and degrees). The emphasis shifts from learning for the genuine love of the subject, to learning for' social worth, market value, rewards and incentives. This is not to say that we should do away with rewards and incentives, but we as individuals and a collective society are in trouble if it becomes the sole end of learning.

Many of us also assume that learning stops when we complete school or university. In our current paradigm, learning is seen as being done mostly in an organised setting, where we learn skills that mostly prepare us for a job. It means a formal education in subjects such as physics, chemistry, biology and so forth. In this environment, learning is connected with skills, facts and figures. But learning, as understood by Gandhi, was much larger and more holistic; it certainly included skills and knowledge, but also went much beyond that. Learning, for Gandhi, became synonymous with living. Learning became a state of mind, an orientation towards life.

People like Gandhi are tremendous learners outside the school or university setting. (He was a pretty good student, even in law school.) He attempted to learn from all his experiences, and hence proactively undertook experiments. He created his own classroom, so to speak, and allowed life to teach and tutor him. He carried out experiments with diet, exercise, celibacy, principles of right conduct and right speech, and experiments in the application of such spiritual principles as non-violence and simplicity. In fact, he called his autobiography *The Story of My Experiments with Truth,* because he felt that his life consisted of nothing but such experiments.

Take the following example: when Gandhi was in South Africa and his social conscience was just beginning to flower, he came across a book that was to have a lasting and profound influence on his life. It was John Ruskin's *Unto This Last.* He read it on a train journey, and was overwhelmed by what he read.

The book reflected to Gandhi some of his own deeply-held convictions. The book spoke about the value of living a simple life, and how one's own highest good comes from striving for the good of one's fellow beings. Gandhi was profoundly moved by what he read, but he did not stop at merely finishing the book. He actually went out and created an environment where he could apply and experiment with what he had learned therein. Thus, Gandhi soon started the Phoenix farm in South Africa. It was an experimental community, made up of a diverse group of Britons, South Africans and Indians. It was here that he put the ideas of Ruskin into practice such as service to others, equality, the dignity of labour etc. He learned much from these experiences, and as such they, in turn, helped him immensely when he led the independence struggle in India.

The great wisdom traditions have spoken of life as a journey — a journey towards greater maturity, self-awareness and growth. Gandhi himself viewed the journey towards self-awareness as more of a path than a goal. He saw learning as a direction, rather than a specific destination. For him, self-discovery was an unfolding, continuous and never-ending work-in-progress. In the introduction to his autobiography, Gandhi writes,

> *I have gone through deep self-introspection, searched myself through and through, and examined and analysed every psychological situation. Yet I am far from claiming any fallibility about my conclusions.*[1]

When the Indian sage, J. Krishnamurthi, started a school along with the British novelist Aldous Huxley, their school motto was *Aun Aprendo* (which is Latin for "I am still learning").[2] The greatest among us have sought to live their lives in that profound spirit; it is this attitude — this learning orientation — that kept Gandhi productive and creative until the end of his life. As he grew older, he became *more* creative, not less. Some of Gandhi's major achievements in political and social fields came when he was in his sixties and later. The epic Dandi march, one of the most remarkable events in the history of modern India, happened when he was 61. The fasting in Calcutta, as well as the "village-a-day pilgrimage" (where he walked 178 miles to stop communal riots) happened when he was 77. He was writing, editing, fasting, travelling and experimenting right to the end of his life. Similarly, the brilliant German poet, author and philosopher Johann von Goethe finished his most famous and critically acclaimed work, *Faust*, at the ripe old age of 82. Michelangelo and Leonardo Da Vinci kept churning out prodigious, highly creative works well into old age.

27

Balancing Action and Reflection

It is commonplace for us, especially in the west, to confuse busyness with effectiveness. However, oftentimes, when we are tremendously busy and caught up in a hectic activity and have no time for reflection, it is then that we are the least effective. We are prone to thinking that those who are busy are "living" their lives, but activity can often become a ruse — a distraction that one uses to escape from oneself, to avoid thinking about the larger purpose in his or her life. In order to be truly effective, one must strike a crucial balance between action and reflection. Both are equally important: action without reflection is dangerous, and reflection without action is useless. The only way we can learn from our mistakes is through reflection. When we act blindly and without understanding the consequences of our actions, we may end up causing a great deal of damage to ourselves and others. At the same time, one cannot reflect and contemplate all the time, if there is no activity or experience to reflect upon.

Meditation and contemplation are extremely important activities, because they create an inner haven of peace and quiet. It is at these times we become most receptive to our sub-consciousness. Many creators and inventors often speak of a creative breakthrough that came to them when they were sitting or lying down quietly. It is only through reflection that many have had their epiphanies or genuine insights. Reflection is also required in order to clarify and define our values, goals, purpose and mission in life. Finally, reflection is necessary if we want to learn from our actions.

Gandhi considered himself a man of action. He said that action was his domain. But he regularly took time out for the renewal of mind, body and spirit. He undertook activities such as prayer, meditation, chanting, and reading inspirational and spiritual texts such as the Bhagavad-Gita, the Sermon on the Mount and the Koran. All these activities energised his spirit and braced him for the challenges of the day ahead. He also spent a lot of time writing journals, which is a powerful reflective activity. He would also spin a charka, which, for Gandhi, was also a form of meditation. All these were powerful strategies for self-renewal. These exercises made him very alert and refreshed. He became centred and aware. Through these exercises, his heart became an oasis of peace that enabled him to deal with the frenzied world outside. He also fasted on a regular basis and tried different types of diet, such as fruit juices and fresh fruits. He walked long distances regularly, and spent time with nature. All of these activities are deeply spiritual exercises that put him in touch with the mysteries of the universe. As Gandhi wrote, *when I admire the wonder of a·sunset or the beauty of the moon, my soul expands in the worship of the Creator.[1]* Through these exercises, he brought a high level of mindfulness to all the activities of his life. He was fully present, aware and awake for every activity.

One of the most extraordinary events in the history of modern India was the "salt march" of 1930. It is widely considered to be the key turning point in the Indian freedom struggle. It was through this event that Gandhi managed to mobilise and unite Indians as one collective force, and it brought the Indian freedom struggle to the world's attention. The creative and highly original idea for this event, which was the brainchild of Gandhi, came to him during a period of quiet and reflection. Although, the nation was restless, and the youth around the country were beginning to get impatient for freedom, Gandhi did not get excited and rush into action. Rather, he cloistered himself, and turned his searchlight within. He spent his days in prayer and silence, and spun the charka. He listened to his conscience, and reflected and contemplated deeply on past experiences and the larger purpose of the struggle; from this period of quiet and peace came the idea for the Salt March.

28

A Holistic Spirituality

One cannot do right in one area of life whilst he is occupied in doing wrong in another; Life is one indivisible whole.[1]

- M.K. Gandhi

For Gandhi, spirituality was not separated from his everyday life or his day-to-day affairs. It was not something he compartmentalised and put into a separate container, so to speak. His spirituality was inextricably intertwined with his everyday activities. It drove everything that he did — all of his actions.

According to Gandhi, one had to seek God by actively engaging with life, and by grappling with everyday problems and challenges. God was not found separate from life, but through family life, work life, relationships, everyday actions, thoughts and attitudes. Truth had to be found by living truly. There is no path separate from life; life is the path. The spiritual journey has to begin from where we are, from *here* and *now*. The joys and disappointments, the pleasures and pain — they are all part of the path. He saw it all as one whole, meaningful entity, and he did not dichotomise and divide life. According to Gandhi, a commitment to truth, ethics and excellence is not just reserved for a few select areas of our life — it must be reflected in *everything* we say and do.

There is an "interconnectedness" to life that is seldom apparent on the surface of our own lives. We think of life in terms of containers, and we tend to compartmentalise life into work, play, family, spiritual matters, social events, and so forth. We tend to think that each of these compartments is isolated from the others in watertight ways — where what we do in one box won't change or affect the others. For example, we think what we do at work does not affect us at home, and vice versa. But ultimately they both are interconnected: any toxicity in our professional life will spill over into our personal lives, and deeply affect our families; the opposite also holds true. Similarly, when our home life is happy and blissful, we find that we have more energy and resilience in our work life.

There is a certain dichotomy among many people who consider themselves deeply religious. Their religiosity shows up only in certain activities, such as visiting churches, temples or mosques, eating certain kinds of food, fasting or dressing in a certain manner. In their day-to-day lives and in their everyday interactions, however, many show no religiosity at all. Their attitudes and behaviours often do not reflect the true principles of love, compassion and brotherhood that are at the heart of all religions. Their behaviour may even show hatred or intolerance towards people of other faiths, or just about anybody who does not agree with their worldview. They may display a "holier than thou," self-righteous attitude toward others. To Gandhi, merely visiting temples or churches, reading spiritual books or chanting the name of God was not synonymous with spirituality. One could do all those things and yet be immature and not understand the true essence of religion.

Gandhi refused to fragment and compartmentalise his life into neat little categories. He did not divide and dichotomise life into work and play, job and home, personal and spiritual, etc. He held a systems approach to life where life was an integrated whole that was indivisible. As he said,

I claim that human mind or human society is not divided into watertight compartments called social, political and religious. All act and react upon one another.[2] He felt that there could be no line drawn between ethics and politics, or between spirituality and business. Life comes to us whole but we tend to fragment it. It is an illusion to think that it can be divided and separated.

29

Learning from Death

Throughout the whole of life, one must continue to learn how to live, and what will amaze you even more, throughout life one must learn to die.

- Seneca (5 BC–65 AD)

For many of us, the notion of our death exists only as an abstract idea—we are only dimly aware of our own imminent death. We live our lives as if we will be on this planet forever, when the reality is that our time here is very limited.

The idea that we will, sooner or later, be dead seems to be an uncomfortable realisation. But there are many good and wonderful things that death can teach us. It is in the contemplation of our death that we can truly learn the value of life. By understanding and grasping the truth that one day we will be no more, our lives and our time on earth becomes more precious. We realise that there are places to visit, people to meet, relationships to mend, potentials to realise and dreams to live. It enables us to quit wasting our time and move on to more important meaningful tasks that we often put on hold for "later."

Socrates stated that one of his main jobs as a philosopher was to reproach people for *undervaluing the greater and overvaluing the lesser*. This is, in many ways, the challenge we all face. What are the things we value most in our lives? Do we assign to them the correct value — the value that it truly deserves? What is the value we place on material wealth, fame, public opinion and power, and what is the value we place on relationships, community, legacy, service, self-expression, and being a part of something larger then we are? Most of us make that seminal mistake, and it is this for which Socrates reproached people: we undervalue the greater and overvalue the lesser.

However, awareness of our finite nature and mortality enables us to affix the correct value to things. This is why Socrates also taught that we should *always be occupied in the practice of dying.* There is a very direct connection here: when we truly understand and grasp the fact that we have a limited time on this planet, we will no longer undervalue the greater and overvalue the lesser. The idea of our death, when deeply contemplated upon, will truly trivialise the trivial — it essentially shines light on the trivial pursuits of our lives.

Some might say that it is impossible for us to contemplate on our own death, or some might say that it is too scary a thought to face up to. But we can most certainly study the lives of those around us and seek to learn from them. Let us examine what happens when people are about to die: no individual on their deathbed speaks of the arguments they won, or the material wealth they accumulated. Invariably, they almost always speak of the rewarding feeling of deep, intimate relationships, genuine friendships, the kindnesses of strangers, etc. No individual has ever said that they wished that they had spent more time at the office. Even when they speak of work, they speak of relationships, people they have touched and affected, and those by whom they have been touched and affected. They tend to speak of meaningful and rewarding tasks that they accomplished in a team.

Regrets almost always involve not telling somebody about how much they loved them or friendships that were lost due to petty differences and fights. They regret the unspoken words, the chances missed to heal wounds. That is why great spiritual masters and philosophers have spoken of the importance of being aware of our imminent death. Buddha said that "death" was his greatest teacher. Socrates, as already mentioned, taught that we should *always be occupied in the practice of dying*, and Gandhi stated that we should *Live as if [we] were to die tomorrow and Learn as if [we] were to live forever.*

Gandhi did not take his life for granted. He was well aware that he was here, on this planet, for only a limited time. In fact, he was reminded of it many times because he had several close calls with death, due to assassination attempts, illnesses and his many fasts unto death. By being aware of his impending death, he lived fully and consciously. He assigned the right value to the right things, and he did not overvalue the lesser and undervalue the greater. He took his own advice and lived his life to the fullest, as if he were going to die tomorrow. Rather than repressing thoughts of death away from his awareness, he tried to be *more* fully aware of it. In his own words, "Life becomes liveable only to the extent that death is treated as a friend, never as an enemy".[1] Socrates meant essentially the same thing, centuries earlier, when he said, "Those of us who think death is an evil are in error". Hence many philosophers have stated that when we turn away from facing our deaths, we also turn away from living our lives more fully.

In fact, when some people are given the news that they have a life-threatening illness and that they may not live for too long, their reactions are very surprising. Although initially they may show feelings of depression, resentment and anger, slowly they begin to show a sense of relief. They sometimes even become thankful for their illness, because it has helped them open their eyes and realise what things truly matter in their lives. They state that they have quit worrying about the artificial and inflated goals that they had been chasing, and they mention that their illness gave them a chance to get off the treadmill of everyday "busyness." They stop running the "rat race," leave behind the addiction of accumulating more and more material goods, and begin to follow their dreams. They start mending relationships, spending more time with loved ones, and learn to forgive and stop holding grudges. They take more time to "smell the roses," watch sunsets, and so forth. In this sense, the news of their impending death, delivered to them by their doctor, turns out to be a blessing in disguise. They feel that they have been given a precious second chance.

Of course, this does not mean that we should wish for a life-threatening illness in our own lives, but when we regularly contemplate on our limited time on this planet, we will be better able to prioritise our activities and our time according to what matters most to us. We will say and do those things that are most deeply meaningful to us, and we will no longer be complacent about going after our dreams. We will learn to live each moment, each hour and each day more mindfully, and more consciously. Such a regular contemplation forces us to re-examine our priorities, and it is an exercise that gives us the opportunity to deal with unfinished business here and now, rather than putting, it off for a "later" that might very well never come. Therapists and religious guides who work with terminally-ill clients say that the number one regret that people have on their death bed is unfinished business such as unfulfilled dreams, unresolved conflicts, meaningful things not done and words not spoken.[2]

Some might say that these are all clichés and platitudes, but if they seem that that way, it is only because they are true.

The truth of these statements is grasped as we grow older and as we move closer to our own impending deaths.

Rather than resisting the idea of death, when we become more conscious and accepting of that fact — when we treat death as a friend — then we can quit wasting our time in being preoccupied with the past or worried about the future. We' can start doing the things that truly matter to us, here and now, and enjoy that process. We learn that the present moment is a precious gift that must be savoured, and we will no longer put life "on hold"; we learn to live fully in the moment. As Zen Master Wu-men (1183-1260) said, *If your mind isn't clouded by unnecessary things, this is the best season of your life.*

30

The Power of Surrender

Since time immemorial, humanity has intuited the presence
of a greater entity that is beyond the reach of its everyday
awareness. It has been variously called God, Brahman,
Allah, Yahweh, The One, Ultimate Reality, Universal
Mind, Buddha Nature, The Tao, etc. Historians and
anthropologists point out that they have yet to come across
a single culture in the past or present that did or does not
believe in some sort of higher power. Archaeologists have
noted that religious artefacts are the oldest artefacts to have
been unearthed; their very survival point to how highly
esteemed they were. Human beings, throughout all ages and
all cultures, have attempted to capture this spiritual reality
in poetic words, personify it through deities, symbolise
it through art, celebrate it through song and dance, and
commune with it through meditation and prayer.

Gandhi believed in such a power. He called his whole life
a search whereupon he sought *to see God face to face*. He
felt an intrinsic sense of connection to this source, and
deeply trusted and surrendered to it. It was by yielding to
this force that he derived his power. This is another one of
life's great paradoxes: his strength came from yielding. He
emerged victorious because he surrendered. We tend think
of surrender as a sign of weakness, but in Gandhi's case,
his "surrender" unleashed his creative energies.

One of the reasons why Alcoholics Anonymous has been
so successful and effective in helping people recover from
alcohol addiction — while more expensive psychiatric

treatments have often failed — is because one of the first steps in AA is to acknowledge the existence of a higher power and then to surrender to it. In Step Three of AA, one makes the decision to turn one's will and life over to the care of "God," however one may understand that term. Paradoxically, in admitting their weakness, they gain their strength.

Willpower and Willingness

Most of us are aware of will power. We are told that by using our will power, we can overcome any obstacle or achieve anything we want. Will power usually implies a "take charge" attitude, but as important as will power is, it is still only half the picture. The other half is the willingness to submit, submission to the Universal Intelligence.

Gandhi had an indomitable will, but it was derived from his willingness to submit to a greater force. At times Gandhi made things happen, but at other times he *allowed* them to happen. Many times, he stood up and took charge, but at other times he just *let go*, went with *the flow* and was content to just *be*. Great people like Gandhi, Emerson and Thoreau strike a crucial balance between these sets of poles: being and doing, resisting and opening, willing and accepting, fighting and surrendering, grasping and letting go. As LaoTzu wrote, *The way to do is to be.* This is by far the most difficult thing to do in our culture, which is obsessed with control and certainty.

There is a time for struggle, for going against the tide, for using will power, for having single-minded focus, for pushing forward with an indomitable will. However, there are times when it is appropriate to let go, to allow, to trust and surrender, and to be receptive. Gandhi's life was full of both sides. No doubt, there were many times and moments in Gandhi's life when he displayed amazing will power. At the same time, however, there were many times and moments when Gandhi knew the wisdom of *allowing*, or just *being.* He displayed openness, willingness and an attitude of surrender to a higher power. That is why there was a certain effortlessness in many of the things that Gandhi did. People marvelled at the effortless ease and natural spontaneity with which he could accomplish complex tasks, but this was the organic result of being in harmony, in tune and in sync with the Intelligence of the universe. In the *Tao Te Ching*, the religious book of Taoism, Lao Tzu refers to this way of accomplishing things as "effortless effort" (*Wu wei*).

Compare this "effortless effort" now with the life that the average human being leads. It is always one of constant striving, struggling, grasping and controlling. Why this huge difference? This is because most of us operate from a deep-rooted assumption that we are separate from nature, the cosmos, the universe and this higher Intelligence. In direct contrast, the sage, the mystic and the saint operate from the understanding that the powerful Intelligence that migrates birds and causes buds to blossom into flowers, seeds to sprout into trees and planets to orbit the sun is not separate from us but is intimately *intertwined* with us. This awe-inspiring intelligence not only works outside of us, but works *within* us and *through* us. We are inextricably linked to it. In fact, the very meaning of the word "religion" is "to rebind," and religion in its deepest sense means to reconnect, and to heal the split between the world, this Intelligence and oneself. It means to reunite with a larger whole — a greater, more meaningful whole. Because saints, sages and mystics feel this sense of belonging to a benevolent force, they do not feel that they work alone in the world; rather, they are working with an infinitely creative source that has their well-being in its heart. It is this trust that engenders their hope, optimism and patience.

The tragedy of exclusively focusing on will power, struggling and pushing is that it is a lopsided, narrow and one- dimensional way of functioning. It also often comes with a serious price: the individual may accomplish what he or she wants, but it comes at the cost of one's physical and emotional health. One's close relationships can also suffer. The feeling that one is constantly swimming upstream and going against the tide will, sooner or later, takes its toll. We burn out and are left feeling drained, frustrated and resentful. It deeply impacts one's sense of hope, optimism, trust, sense of belonging and self-esteem.

But when one is using willpower in conjunction with "willingness," then there is an acknowledgement of a greater force, a greater intelligence that is guiding us. One aligns and attunes oneself to that force. This act of trusting something larger than oneself gives one a state of calmness and peace of mind. Even if events do not go as planned or as we imagined they would, there is still something to be learned from them. The attitude here is that the Universe knows best, and it may be guiding us along a path.

When people thus surrender, they shift to a higher order of effectiveness and creativity. Their lives become a vehicle of expression for something greater and higher. These people become an instrument through which a greater force unfolds itself and shows itself to the world. It is best expressed in the Biblical saying, *Thy will, not mine.* Joseph Jaworski calls it *the capacity to participate in... an unfolding creative order[1]*. We become the co-creators as we participate in shaping our future, both personal and collective, rather than merely reacting to the outside events that impinge upon us.

This state has been termed as "being in a state of grace," whereupon meaningful coincidences begin to occur. Things begin to fall into place, almost mysteriously. Doors begin to open up where none existed before. In such moments, we see with great certainty and clarity that we are headed along the right path. We feel guided along the path by a force that is bigger and beyond us. Carl Jung studied this phenomenon, and called it "synchronicity," and when it happens, there is a natural rhythm to one's life, as if one is taking part in the most profoundly moving symphony.

Trust is a casualty in today's hyper-competitive world. Even in relationships, trust does not develop overnight or immediately. In relationships, trust is built slowly — and so it is with our trust in life, too. It is not an overnight exercise; we cannot deeply mistrust life one day and trust it wholeheartedly the next. It is a slow process and we may need to cultivate it consciously. Gandhi continually sought to strengthen this trust in the cosmos by getting in touch with the life-source through prayers, contemplation, and days of silence, fasting, and even spinning the charka. He also spent a lot of time reading and learning from the spiritual texts such as the Bhagavad-Gita and the Sermon on the Mount.

When we bring this aspect of trust and surrender into our lives, we can ease up on our exclusive dependence on will power. We can use will power *in conjunction with* our intuitive wisdom. This way of first trusting and surrendering to a greater power — and then allowing it to work through us — is a far greater and more superior way of working than to merely manipulate one's will power. Surrender is the way of those who trust in the cosmos; they align, attune and harmonise themselves with a Benevolent Power that they believe stands on the side of the just, the good and the compassionate.

31

The Importance of Problems and Challenges

A gem cannot be polished without friction, nor a man perfected without trials...Difficulties strengthen the mind, as labour does the body.

- Seneca (5 BC–65 AD)

One of the major ways in which life teaches us is through the problems and challenges we face. It is in great part due to the challenges in our life that we grow, mature and become self-aware. The critical moments in our life hold the most valuable lessons for us. Although we would all like life to unfold in a linear, predictable, and smooth manner with no rude surprises, such a life would simply be too boring and unfulfilling.

Problems are our wake up calls. We seldom choose to learn, grow and mature voluntarily and of our own accord. We prefer instead to stay ensconced within our comfort zone, in our protective shell. In these moments, problems and challenges act as catalysts, shaking us out of our complacency and pushing us towards growth. As Benjamin Franklin once said, *those things that hurt, instruct.* Similarly, in the Chinese language, the symbol for "crisis' is a combination of the symbols for "danger" and "opportunity". The ancient Chinese, in developing the symbols of their language, seemed to have had an intuitive understanding that our stumbling blocks can also be our stepping stones towards maturity and wisdom.

By actively confronting and solving our problems, we grow mentally, emotionally and spiritually. It is through this process that we gain our wisdom. Yet, many of us actively attempt to avoid our problems, rather than face up to them. We would rather let things drift along, happy with the *status quo.* The process goes something like this: When the significant crisis or problem comes knocking at our door, our first line of defence is denial and/or distraction. Most of us, most of the time, attempt to deny, avoid or disown our problems. We refuse to take responsibility, or we attempt to downplay the depth and seriousness of the problem. If we are forced to acknowledge the problem, we then hope that the problem will go away on its own — somehow miraculously disappear by itself. If that does not work, and the problem continues to exist, we then opt for short cuts, quick fixes, and easy solutions. We use the "band-aid and aspirin" approach, which treats the symptoms; this may give us a temporary respite, but it leaves the underlying cause untouched. We tend to "solve" the symptoms, and not the disease. Only when we realise that none of these really work, do we then seek genuine growth — and by facing up to the challenge, we take a serious step on the road to self-discovery.

The best example of boldly facing up to a challenge comes to us from the life of the Buddha. Before he was venerated with the title of "Buddha" (coming from the root word 'Budh' which means awakened), he was Prince Gautama, heir to the throne of a kingdom in northern India. He had been brought up amidst great wealth and opulence, and lived a protected life with every pleasure at his beck and call. He grew Up within the palace walls, having no contact with the outside world. But on his first visit outside the palace gates, he came face-to-face with the harsh realities of death, disease and pain. He could not get these haunting sights out of his mind. They opened up some deep questions and doubts within him, but rather than ignoring them through distractions, he decided to deal with them at a fundamental level. Leaving the palace and his princely life behind, he wandered the jungles of India, meeting and practicing with wandering yogis, seeking and searching for the meaning of life. After six years of intensive and single-minded seeking and learning, he is said to have attained enlightenment beneath the Bodhi tree.

In fact, all the wisdom traditions have long recognised the invaluable contributions of pain and challenges to a person's spiritual growth towards greater maturity and self-awareness. Indeed, the clarion call that has issued forth from every one of the great traditions is to *know thyself.* This is the path to enlightenment, and it is often initiated through encountering problems, challenges and suffering. As the Danish philosopher Sören Kierkegaard puts it,

A man may perform astonishing feats and comprehend a vast amount of knowledge, and yet have no understanding of himself. But suffering directs a man to look within. If it succeeds, then there, within him, is the beginning of his learning.

Great people such as Gandhi understand intuitively the value of pain, problems and challenges. They see the intricate connection between pain and growth, and they see challenges as ideal opportunities for widening the consciousness. Hence, we notice a consistent tendency among these people to welcome rather than avoid challenges. They put themselves in new situations, actively seek new experiences, meet with new people and try new things. They actively shoulder responsibilities, rather than shirking them.

32

The Value of Role Models and Mentors

Keep away from people who belittle your ambitions. Small people always do that, but the really great make you feel that you, too, can become great.

-Mark Twain (1835-1910)

Gandhi sought and found mentors from whom he could learn, and with whom he could discuss his doubts and dilemmas. He pro-actively sought their guidance and counsel on spiritual and political issues. He learned valuable lessons from each of them, and they all added to his personal and spiritual development.

As a child, Gandhi was deeply affected by a fictional play called Harishchandra. The central character in this story is a truthful man, and although he goes through many ordeals, trials and tribulations, he never wavers from telling the truth. Gandhi was profoundly influenced by this story; this ideal of upholding the truth was one that inspired him greatly, and it became a central component in his own life. Although Gandhi knew that Harishchandra was a fictional character, he became a "living reality."[1] Harishchandra was Gandhi's first role model.

His first mentor was Raychandbhai, a diamond merchant by profession, but more importantly, a man of impeccable character and integrity —qualities that deeply appealed to Gandhi. He was also a deeply spiritual person, and his life revolved around spirituality rather than his business. He had a tremendous knowledge of the scriptures of Hinduism and Jainism. Gandhi went to him to clarify his doubts and have discussions on religious issues. Gandhi wrote that in times of spiritual crisis, Raychandbhai was his refuge.[2]

Similarly, in his early political life, Gandhi had a mentor named Gokhale from whom he learned much about politics. Once again, Gandhi was attracted to him mainly because Gokhale was a truthful, honest and sincere person. Gandhi writes in his autobiography that in their very first meeting, Gokhale had won his heart.[3] When Gandhi returned to India from South Africa, it was Gokhale who suggested that Gandhi take an entire year off from politics and simply tour the country, so that he could know India more intimately. Gandhi accepted the advice and travelled the length and breadth of India by rail — and, in the process, learning much in that year.

Gandhi also corresponded with Leo Tolstoy of Russia, when Tolstoy was in the twilight of his life. Gandhi was deeply moved by Tolstoy's book, *The Kingdom of God is Within You*. In this book, Tolstoy detailed what was, according to him, the true message of Jesus. Tolstoy expressed his core philosophy thus: love is the "highest and indeed the only law of life." He also severely criticised the religious and social institutions which, in his opinion, were perverting and twisting the teachings of Jesus. He felt that nothing will really change in society until there is an inner moral revolution in each person. Gandhi was impressed by the "independent thinking, profound morality, and the truthfulness" of this book, and Gandhi credits Tolstoy's book for making him a firm believer in ahimsa (the power of non-violence).[4]

Gandhi wrote to Tolstoy, explaining that he had been profoundly affected by Tolstoy's book, and that he was now applying Tolstoy's teachings and suggestions to the non-violent struggle in South Africa. Gandhi's exposure to Tolstoy's ideas and their correspondence came at a pivotal time in Gandhi's life. Gandhi had just started the civil disobedience movement in South Africa; he lacked political experience and the whole method of Satyagraha was still in its embryonic stage. Tolstoy, through his letters, encouraged Gandhi and affirmed that Gandhi was headed along the right path. In Tolstoy's last letter to him, he stated, *Your activity (of non-violent resistance) is the most essential work, the most important of all the work now being done in the world.*[5]

Role models, guides and mentors play a crucial role in our growth and development. They are our reminders of greatness. They remind us that we can be bigger, larger and better than we currently are. Rather than horde it, good mentors share their hard-won wisdom with their students. They are wise and trustworthy counsellors who can offer valuable advice when we feel stuck or confused, or are at a crossroads in life. Most importantly, they teach not solely through their words, but rather through their actions. They teach by *who they are*. In the above examples, Gandhi was deeply impacted not only by the advice that these men gave him but, more importantly, by the quality of their character.

33

The Importance of a Sense of Humour

Gandhi had a sense of humour that allowed him to laugh at himself. This is one of the aspects of Gandhi that is lesser-known to the outside world. Those people who had the privilege of meeting him and working with him describe that he had an amazing sense of humour, and an ability to laugh at himself. People assume that because he was dealing with challenges of such overwhelming magnitude, that he would be a very serious person. On the contrary: he had a sense of humour that put others at ease and made him fun to be around. Here is one example of his sense of humour: when Gandhi was invited to Buckingham Palace to meet with the King, Gandhi went in his loincloth. Later, when he was asked if he was not a bit underdressed for the occasion, he replied with his characteristic wit, "His Majesty had on enough clothes for the both of us!".

Sense of humour, however, is not just about making witty remarks. It implies an ability to laugh at oneself, and to not take one's self too seriously all the time. It is said that laughter has a healing effect on us, because it releases endorphins that strengthen our immune system. The average child is said to laugh 300 times a day, but as we grow older, we tend to laugh less and less. (This is sad, because laughter relieves stress, smoothes tension and may even provide creative inspiration.)

Humour and laughter added to Gandhi's positive and hopeful attitude. He would poke fun at himself. He took his job and his mission very seriously, but not himself. It would not be a stretch to say that his sense of humour helped him to overcome adversity. As he himself said, *If I had no sense of humour, I would long ago have committed suicide.*

34

The Power of Prioritising

Simplicity, simplicity, simplicity! I say, let your affairs be as two or three, and not a hundred or a thousand; instead of a million, count half a dozen, and keep your account on your thumbnail.

- Henry David Thoreau (1817–1863)

Gandhi focused on what he felt was essential. He undertook a few important, core activities and disregarded the rest. He prioritised his tasks and roles in their order of importance. As Goethe stated, *Things which matter most must never be at the mercy of things which matter least.*

In our modern lives, we face levels of rush and pressure that are unprecedented. There are too many conflicting concerns, too many demands, and we often commit ourselves to too many projects. The wise Stoic philosopher Seneca, who lived more than two millennia ago, called this "busy idleness," because although the person may be busy, they are accomplishing very little of value. Moreover such a life, more often than not, results in stress and burnout. When we live such frenzied lives and are distracted by a myriad of tasks and roles, we deny ourselves the tranquillity of mind and a sense of fulfilment that comes from having accomplished something that truly, deeply matters to us.

Knowing what was important, Gandhi began to focus on those things: spiritual growth, service to others and character development became his fundamental priorities.

There was a direct correlation between the activities he undertook every day and his ultimate purposes and values. They were in harmony. He did not do a million different things, but chose instead a few tasks and did them well. He brought his focus and concentration to bear upon these few, essential activities. In a Business Week interview, Steve Jobs (the CEO of Apple) stated, *it is only by saying 'no' that you can concentrate on the things that are really important.* He considered this principle one of the reasons for innovation at Apple.[1] Indeed, as psychologist William James remarked, *The essence of genius is to know what to overlook.*

In order to be truly effective, our activities must be consistent with the things that we value most in our lives. These deserve our highest priority.

35

Trusteeship

Gandhi did not seek ownership of wealth, property or titles. He was not about ownership, but rather stewardship. In the final analysis, he saw himself as a caretaker: he was a custodian, a trustee entrusted with responsibilities to care for his fellow beings. In Gandhi's worldview, we are born with the distinct responsibility to care for and tend to all the assets put under our responsibility, for the larger good of the earth community (both human and non-human).

This idea of "trusteeship" was deeply connected to Gandhi's spirituality, but there was a practical component to it as well. When we behave from a sense of ownership or entitlement, we feel that we have a right and privilege over nature, and nature is then seen only as a resource. We behave as if nature exists to serve our purpose — it is seen as being here for our benefit only. Because we as humans tend to see most things only through the lens of what its usefulness is to us, such a view or attitude invariably leads to excess and exploitation.

But Gandhi saw things differently. He saw the planet and all of its inhabitants as sacred and precious beyond any worldly scale of valuation. According to him, there is an inherent sacredness to the natural world, to the biosphere. Gandhi understood that there is an intrinsic value to nature and its animals and plants, beyond the monetary value imposed upon them by humans. This requires a profound shift in our consciousness, whereupon we see the earth as more than a resource, and instead see it as inherently and innately valuable, in and of itself.

To provide an analogy that will help us put this in perspective, what if we were to ask parents, "What is the monetary value of your children?" Most parents would be aghast at such a question; the very notion sounds absurd. We do not see our children in terms of monetary value, nor would we intentionally set out to use them as a "resource" for our own selfish ends. To parents, children are endowed with an infinite worth that is beyond measurement in monetary or economic terms. In India, there is a wonderful saying that helps us understand the concept of infinite worth. It says that *The rest of the world may think that a crow is ugly, but to the crow, nobody is as beautiful and precious as her own offspring.* Gandhi's ideal was to expand this same thinking to all people on this planet, and also to our natural world. The Lebanese poet Khalil Gibran wrote this piece of advice for parents, which I think expresses Gandhi's concept of trusteeship well.

> *Your children are not your children.*
> *They are the sons and daughters of Life's longing for itself.*
> *They come through you but not from you,*
> *And though they are with you, yet they belong not to you.*

According to Gandhi, though the earth and all of her beautiful creations are with us, they do not belong to us. In fact, he even went so far as to argue that no one really owned anything, and that people were only the "trustees" of things. He understood that in order to live, we as human beings had to use and consume some things in nature such as soil, water, plants, animals and so forth. But as trustees, it becomes necessary for us to use them in such a way that does not abuse them, lead to waste or diminish it for future generations. Each individual or community could take only what they needed and leave the rest to be — and even that act of taking is done with a profound sense of gratitude and thankfulness. Many of the Aboriginal and

North American Indian tribes have lived with this profound sense of harmony, where even when an animal was killed in order to be eaten, the tribe members offered thanks to the animal for having given its life to feed the tribe, and they also prayed for the animal's soul. Every part of that animal would then be used in some way, so that nothing would be wasted — even the bones, claws and blood would be used to make crafts and artefacts.

It was precisely because of his deeply-held belief and conviction in the notion of trusteeship that Gandhi also went on to progressively simplify his life. The more we simplify our wants the more we can share with others, and the less we will use from nature. In his words, *Live simply so that others may simply live.*

This is not to say that we must completely disregard or ignore money or monetary value. Money is a medium of exchange, and it is important to understand that we, as a society, have chosen it as such. It is a social "contract," or a rule that we have all accepted so that transactions can be made more easily. The economic value of an item is something we, as a society, have mutually agreed to imbue on an item, and we have thus chosen to make it "real." But that is not the *only value* that item has. At any given point in time we can choose to look deeper and see an item through our spiritual lens, rather than simply looking at everything through our economic lens.

The current economic paradigm that we are pursuing places primary importance on the economic market, and not on the biosphere or nature. Economic growth has become the be-all and end-all, and it is seen as a panacea — the cure for all of our ills. Ecologists, environmentalists and many scientists unanimously agree that economic activity, as pursued in its current form, is *fundamentally incompatible with ecological or biological sustainability on a finite earth.*[1] Due in large part to our notion of ownership, this sense of entitlement combined with greed, we have managed to place the health, survival and the continued viability of the biosphere in jeopardy. In the past, we tended to believe that when it comes to the environment, we could live without regard for the consequences of our behaviour. We have been reckless in consuming natural resources, as if they would last forever. We have polluted the air, water and land — the entire ecosystem. We have managed to 'exterminate a significant portion of the animal and plant life on earth in a relatively short period of time. As a species, we are seeking our own pleasures and largely ignoring the needs of other species and future generations. Gandhi was very concerned with the impact that greed, rampant materialism and industrial mass-consumption lifestyles were having on the environment. He summed it up beautifully when he said that *the world has enough for everyone's need, but not enough for everyone's greed.* To him, simple living was sustainable living, but in order to do that we had to first move from being egocentric to eco-centric. We have to shift our view to one where we see ourselves as trustees — custodians who are entrusted with the sacred responsibility of caring for all of earth's wonderful creations.

36

<u>Synergy</u>

Gandhi recognised the deeply interdependent nature of our lives. He was able to see how the individual is part of a wider community, and he was aware of the crucial relationship between "me" and "we." What is this crucial relationship?

One of the first things we notice is that people gain their awareness as people only through interactions with others. We come into this world through another human being, and we survive and grow through the care and nurturance of other human beings. Our consciousness and language is moulded, shaped and formed through interplays with other human beings, and through this very relatedness. Human beings cannot satisfy a single need without the existence of others. As children, we are dependent on others for our food, shelter, physical touch and emotional bonding. As we grow up, our need to belong and our need for self-esteem and self-expression can be satisfied only within a community. Others must acknowledge our existence and achievements, otherwise none of those needs can be satisfied. Simply put, humanness can occur only within a community of human beings. Carl Jung stated it well when he said that *each of us needs others to fully be ourselves.*

The family and the community that nurtures and nourishes us is, in turn, dependent on the biosphere for all its needs. We depend on the environment and the larger ecosystem for our food, water and air — basics without which no human being can survive. We require clean air, water, sunlight, soil and all the other millions of organisms that work in a synergistic manner to make our own existence possible. We thus see that there is an interdependent nature to all of life. We don't live isolated lives; our lives are, from beginning to end, deeply communal. We live in a community of beings, both human and non-human. We are part of a deeply mutual and interdependent network of all life. "I am because we are" is an ancient Hopi saying that recognises this truth. When we deeply contemplate this interdependence and combine it with a growth in our compassion and sensitivity, we start to feel a deep sense of solidarity, of interconnectedness with other human beings — which in turn begins to extend and encompass the animal world and nature in general.

That is why people like Gandhi attempted to grow *with* others and not *at the expense* of others. Having seen and sensed the interdependence of all life, the truly maturing individual attempts to grow through mutual help of each other. For them, life is not a zero-sum game; in order to "win," others don't have to lose. They attempt to grow synergistically, in harmony with others and their environment. The more they win, the more others win. Gandhi used the rich, evocative example of the honeybee to drive home this point: the more nectar a bee collects from flowers, the more it helps out its environment, because it cross-pollinates that many more flowers.

Gandhi realised that *nobody* wins unless *everybody* wins. Thus, for great people, what they truly, deeply want is also good for society at large. It becomes very difficult for us to pinpoint whether they are giving or receiving. Is the honeybee giving or receiving? It is doing both. Giving and receiving thus blend into one seamless whole. Self-actualisers such as Gandhi transcend the dichotomy of selfish and unselfish. What Gandhi wanted for himself was also synergistic, harmonious and beneficial to the world.

People such as Gandhi display what has been termed as "enlightened self-interest": the more they display such self-interest, the more other people benefit, the more the environment benefits, and the more future generations benefit. In the cases of such people, the dichotomy between self and society is transcended, and attempts and intentions to grow in harmony with one's environment is a sign of an ever-increasing awareness, of a deepening and widening of consciousness.

37

"Sarvodaya": "For the Welfare of All"

We are increasingly becoming aware that economic growth, which comes at the cost and expense of leaving others behind, has negative consequences on all of us in the long run. The ever-widening gap between the rich and the poor of the world is alarming. The richest 20 percent of humanity has 82 times the income of the poorest 20 percent — and the top '20 percent consumes 86 percent of the world's resources[1]. The assets controlled by the 200 wealthiest individuals in the world are greater than the Gross Domestic Product of the entire continent of Africa. Just think about that: a mere 200 individuals collectively hold more wealth than an entire continent of 600 million people! Even within countries, there is a huge yawning gap between the rich and the poor. In America, for example, the gap between the wealthiest and the poorest is the highest it has been in 70 years. What is of increasing concern is that this gap is widening, and the trend shows no sign of reversing itself. It is not that the global economy has not grown — indeed, it has grown spectacularly, but the top 20 to 30 percent of income earners have enjoyed virtually all the benefits of that growth.

Gandhi was deeply saddened by these economic systems, which kept large numbers of people chained to poverty while a few enjoyed unparalleled economic wealth. But Gandhi's solution to this problem was not primarily economic. He was not intent upon merely changing the system from the outside by applying communism, capitalism or socialism. Gandhi's solution was primarily moral or spiritual. This is not to say that he neglected the practical side. In fact, he ceaselessly worked to socially uplift the poor and marginalised by helping open small village industries, cooperatives and so forth that encouraged self-sufficiency. But he felt, first and foremost, that effective change would have to come from within one's self, and not be imposed from the outside as a system. Such a revolution had to be in one's own heart and mind; one had to see deeply how a selfish grasping for possessions and moral complacency was contributing to this worldwide injustice, and how it was a violation of one's own deeper self.

In order for such an internal revolution to occur, one has to commit to growth and maturity — emotionally, mentally, morally and spiritually. When thus committed, at some point there is a profound shift of consciousness: as one begins to grow through stringent self-examination and self-discipline, one begins to rid one's self of tendencies for personal aggrandisement, possessiveness, greed and exploitation. As compassion and sensitivity increases, people begin to understand deeply how actions motivated by greed, fear of not having enough or violence not only affect others, but are also hindrances to one's own sense of fulfilment and happiness. One thus begins to live in a way that honours others, the environment and the self. Gandhi called this way of living "Sarvodaya," which means "for the welfare of all." After having lived much of his life according to that principle, Gandhi in the last year of his life expressed his social thoughts thus:

> *I will give you a talisman. Whenever you are in doubt, or when the self becomes too much with you, apply the following test. Recall the face of the poorest and the weakest man [or woman] whom you may have seen, and ask yourself, if the step you contemplate is going to be of any use to him [or her].*

Will he [or she] gain anything by it? Will it restore him [or her] to a control over his [or her] own life and destiny? In other words, will it lead to swaraj [freedom] for the hungry and spiritually starving millions? Then you will find your doubts and your self melt away.[2]

38

"Swaraj"; Freedom and Responsibility

The concept of "Swaraj" is key to understanding Gandhi and his philosophy. In one sense, "Swaraj" simply meant freedom from British rule. In another sense, it also meant a "disciplined rule from within." To Gandhi, mere political freedom was not enough by itself. Gandhi felt that freedom conceived in its narrow sense — as mere political freedom — often degenerates into an unrestrained pursuit of selfish goals at the expense of one's fellow beings. Internal freedom, however, brought true freedom because through it there was freedom from fear, freedom from greed, freedom from prejudice, and freedom from the instinct to aggrandise, dominate and accumulate.

When we lack this inner freedom, mere political freedom is often wasted away or abused. Gandhi began to use the word "Swaraj" to differentiate it from the English terms "freedom" or "independence," because these latter words have no connotation of a sense of responsibility to the one who is free. It focuses on rights, but not on responsibilities. Gandhi, borrowing the term "Swaraj" from the ancient Indian spiritual texts, the Upanishads, defined and interpreted it as external freedom and a "disciplined rule from within." It was freedom *with* self-restraint, and *not* freedom to do as one pleased; nor was it a freedom from all restraint.

No Task is Beneath Us

Gandhi considered no task beneath him (unless it was immoral, unethical or hurtful to others). He met and moved with powerful viceroys and politicians in the highest echelons of power, but he was humble enough to do even the most menial of tasks himself. In his own house and at his ashrams, he would clean the bathrooms when it was his turn. There were many people who would have loved to do this work for him, but he saw the innate dignity of labour. He even felt strongly that undertaking manual labour was good for a person. Gandhi could have spent all his time expounding on his lofty ideals and doing only large tasks, but he had the humility to do many of the most menial tasks. He was consumed by a great vision for all of India, but he also did many day-to-day jobs. As the Indian Yogic sage, Swami Vivekananda stated,

> *If you really want to judge the character of a man, look not at his great performances.... Watch people do their most common actions; those are indeed the things which will tell you their real character....the really great person is one whose character is great always, the same wherever he or she be.*

As a person begins to receive a higher education and become more upwardly mobile, the more they tend to think that certain tasks are somehow beneath them. Some tasks, such people believe, are considered unworthy of them and they think that in doing them, they will somehow lose their status. Of course, many of us do undertake menial tasks in our own households, but we often do so only because we *have* to. If we had the choice, we would rather have somebody else do them for us. But Gandhi believed that no matter how intellectually brilliant a person may be, even that person would gain tremendously by willingly undertaking some manual labour. In his mind, any task that involves the use of one's hands and feet (such as gardening, farming, cleaning, cooking for the family or community, cleaning the surroundings, carpentry and so forth) was good. In this way, one can stay grounded and in touch with the earth and nature; also, when we engage in manual labour, it helps us connect spiritually with the millions of people around the world who earn their honest day's living doing such tasks.

Conclusion: The Hero's Journey

*Each Man had only one genuine vocation — to find
the way to himself.... His task was to discover his
own destiny — not an arbitrary one — and live it out
wholly and resolutely within himself*

- Hermann Hesse, Damien

Joseph Campbell, in his wonderful book *The Hero with a
Thousand Faces*, studies the stories, fairy tales, and myths
of different cultures from different time periods in history.
He found an underlying unity in all these seemingly
different stories. While there were obvious differences in
setting, language, characters and so forth, he found that at
their core, they were the same stories! Every story had a
master template, a common plotline: the Hero (either male
or female) embarked alone on a very difficult journey,
went through many trials and tribulations, and finally won
a decisive victory against overwhelming odds. Campbell
came to call this "the Hero's journey" or the "monomyth"
because it was essentially the same story told in infinite
variations.[1]

Providing examples from different cultures throughout
history, Campbell suggests that the Hero's journey is a
metaphor for what is essentially the journey of every human
being towards great levels of awareness — of one's self,
and of the world. It is the process whereby one awakens
from the "hypnosis of social conditioning." It is a voyage of
growth, maturity and learning and this journey, more often

than not, begins with doubt and fear but paradoxically is also tremendously exciting and ultimately fulfilling.

Both Carl Jung and Joseph Campbell suggest that this myth or archetype is embedded within the collective consciousness of the human psyche. That is why almost every culture, without exception, has the archetype of the Hero in its stories and folklore. All individuals and cultures have an intuitive understanding of the Hero and the Hero's journey. We have seen this perennial plotline repeated ad infinitum in movies, plays and literature. There is a happy ending, but only after the Hero goes through a crisis, weathers the storm and comes out stronger. It is expressed in different ways, such as the hero learning profound life lessons or winning against his or her more powerful evil tormentors, or finding the way home, or winning the love of his or her life. Stories that inspire and uplift us point to the fact that all of us innately and intuitively grasp and understand the significance of the Hero's journey.

We see this myth played out in real life, too. When we look back at the history of our world, we notice that many of the great men and women who have made a positive and long-standing contribution to our world have treaded the same path as the Hero's journey. They too have had to struggle to step out of their slumber, comfort zone or cocoon. They had to face up to their own fears and deepest doubts, and they won decisive victories, both internal and external, against overwhelming odds. Mahatma Gandhi, Helen Keller, Buddha, and Martin Luther King, Jr. are just a few of the inspirational examples who stand as a testimony to the truth of the tale of the Hero's journey.

What the Hero's journey suggests to us is that if we want to learn, grow, mature and truly discover our destiny, then we must embark on our *own* journey. We must become the Hero of our own story. If we want to become our own person — if we want to discover our destiny, our authentic voice — then we must step out of our cocoon. There may be great fear and trepidation, and the feeling of uncertainty that comes from stepping into the great unknown, and into uncharted territory. But it is a risk that we must take, and it is well worth taking.

Those who make this journey often display greater levels of honesty, authenticity, truthfulness, integrity, inclusivity, conscience, and courage than they had before they set out on the said journey. Since time immemorial, some of the world's greatest philosophers, mystics, saints, sages and laypeople have .gone through this journey. They tread on a road less travelled and "march to the beat of a different drum." They have discovered themselves, and in terms of their destiny, they often live and play by their own set of internal rules and standards, which are not only harmonious with their conscience, but is mindful of impacts upon others. As the Buddha said it, *Carpenters bend wood; fletchers bend arrows; wise men fashion themselves.*

They become more effective and fully-integrated human beings who have a certain inner clarity about the principles and virtues they deem worthy and valuable in their lives. They have their own personal credo or personal philosophy, but this inner certainty cannot be arrived at easily. If it is to be authentic, valuable and effective, this certainty comes only through an "inner wrestling." Great leaders and visionaries have all had to go through this essential process of wrestling with their souls; an arduous process of self- discovery and stringent self-examination leading to greater levels of maturity, awareness, harmony and peace. Remember the Hero's journey: first, there is fear; then there is struggle, and only after that is there a happy ending.

In conclusion, I want to say that the goal before us all is very clear. The goal of the Hero's journey is to rise above our small-mindedness, bigotry, intolerance, greed and capacity for cruelty. It is the struggle to find our true calling in life; to rise above the "hypnosis of social conditioning"; to find our own voice; to become ever more truthful, honest, inclusive, just and compassionate; to see the spark of divinity in all beings; and to truly live, love and learn in our limited time on this planet. There is an old Indian saying, which goes thus: *When you were born, you cried and the world rejoiced. Live your life in such a manner that when you die, the world cries and you rejoice.*

I wish you all the very best in your journey towards health, wholeness, wisdom and happiness.

Om Shanthi, Shanthi, Shanthi
(Peace, Peace, Peace unto all)

- The End -

NOTES

Chapter 2: Gandhi: A Brief Biography

1. Mohandas K. Gandhi, *Gandhi: An Autobiography, The Story of my Experiments with Truth.* Reprint Edition. (Boston, Massachusetts: Beacon Press in arrangement with Navajivan Trust, 1993).

2. Ibid.

3. Ibid.

4. Ibid.

5. Ibid.

6. Ibid.

7. This quote is cited in Mohandas K. Gandhi, *Mind of Mahatma Gandhi.* Edited by R.K. Prabhu and U.R. Rao. (Ahmedabad: Navajivan Publishing, 1996). The online version of this book can be viewed at www.mkgandhi.org.

8. Mohandas K. Gandhi, *Gandhi: An Autobiography, The Story of my Experiments with Truth.* Reprint Edition. (Boston, Massachusetts: Beacon Press in arrangement with Navajivan Trust, 1993).

9. Ibid.

10. Ibid.

11. Shashi Tharoor cites this quotation by Nehru in his biography of Nehru, entitled *Nehru: The Invention of India*. (New York: Arcade Publishing, 2003), p. 39.

12. Albert Einstein penned this tribute after Gandhi's death. The complete tribute is available on the web page, www.mkgandhi.org/tributes.

Chapter 3: A Strong Sense of Purpose

1. Abraham Maslow, *The Farther Reaches of Human Nature*. (New York: Penguin Books, 1993), p. 42

2. *George Bernard Shaw, Man and Superman*, Preface (Penguin, 1950).

3. Viktor E. Frankl makes a similar assertion in the preface to his book, *Man's Search for Meaning*. (New York: Touchstone Books, 1984).

4. Ibid

5. See Larry Dossey, *Meaning and Medicine: Lessons from a Doctor's tales of Breakthrough and Healing*. (New York: Bantam Books, 1991), pp 62-63.

6. Researchers initially attributed this finding to biochemical factors such as circadian rhythms. However, this factor alone could not account for the greater occurrences of heart attacks and chest pains on Monday. Larry Dossey suggests that the Black

Monday syndrome occurs more due to emotional and psychological factors such as job dissatisfaction. See Larry Dossey, *Meaning and Medicine: Lessons from a Doctor's tales of Breakthrough and Healing.* (New York: Bantam Books, 1991), pp 62-63.

7. Viktor E. Frankl, Man's Search for Meaning. (New York: Touchstone books, 1984).

8. Ibid.

9. Psychologist Abraham Maslow found that all self-actualizers transcend the work-joy dichotomy. See Abraham Maslow, The Farther Reaches of Human Nature. (New York: Penguin Books, 1993).

Chapter 4: The Importance of Character

1. Stephen R. Covey, *The Seven Habits of Highly Effective People.* (New York: Fireside, Simon and Schuster, 1990), p. 18.

2. This assertion is made by the National Association of Anorexia Nervosa and Associated Disorders in the U.S.A. The information is posted on their web site, www.anad.org.

3. Deepak Chopra, *The Seven Spiritual Laws of Success.* (San Rafael, California: Amber Allen Publishing, 1994).

4. Mohandas K. Gandhi, *Mahatma: Life of Mohandas Karamchand Gandhi.* Edited by D.G. Tendulkar. Volume 2, 2nd Edition. (New Delhi: Publications Division, 1960), p. 376

Chapter 5: The Power of Our Everyday Choices and Actions

1. Jim Collins in his study of how good companies become great found a similar principle at work. None of these companies became "great" overnight. These companies initiated and sustained a quiet, organic process of improvement and development — over a substantial period of time — in one consistent direction thus enabling them to make the leap from good to great. See Jim Collins, *Good to Great.* (New York: Harper Business, HarperCollins Publishers, 2001).

Chapter 6: Intrinsic Sense of Satisfaction

1. This study was done by Mihaly Csikszentmihalyi and is mentioned in the book, Emotional Intelligence. See Daniel Goleman, *Emotional intelligence: Why It Can Matter More Than IQ.* (New York: Bantam Books, 1995).

2. See Mohandas K. Gandhi, *Selections from Gandhi.* Edited by Nirmal Kumar Bose. Revised Edition. (Ahmedabad: Navajivan Trust, 1996). The online version of this book is available at www.mkgandhi.org.

3. Mihaly Csikszentmihalyi, *Flow: The Psychology of Optimal Experience.* (New York: Harper and Row Publishers, 1990)

Chapter 7: Channelizing Anger

1. The comparison of anger to electricity was made by Gandhi in a conversation he had with his grandson,

Arun Gandhi. Arun Gandhi narrates this conversation in an article entitled *Grandfather Gandhi: Peace Was His Way*. The full article can be found on the web site: www.gandhiinstitute.org.

2. Gandhi made these comments on anger in the journal, *Young India*. It is also cited in Mohandas K. Gandhi, *Mind of Mahatma Gandhi*. Edited by R.K. Prabhu and U.R. Rao. (Ahmedabad: Navajivan Publishing, 1996).

Chapter 8: The Power of a Dream

1. Peter Senge, *The Fifth Discipline*: *The Art and Practice of Learning Organizations*. (New York: Currency Doubleday, 1994), p. 209

2. Mohandas K. Gandhi, *Mahatma: Life of Mohandas Karamchand Gandhi*. Edited by D.G. Tendulkar. Volume 4, 2nd Edition. (New Delhi: Publications Division, 1960), p. 165

Chapter 9: The Importance of Risking Failure

1. Jim Collins and Jerry Porras, *Built to Last: The Successful Habits of Visionary Companies*. (New York: HarperCollins Publishers, 1997).

Chapter 10: The Value of Creative Tension

1. Robert Fritz calls this "structural tension" and explains this idea beautifully in his book, *The Path of Least Resistance* and it is a must-read for anyone who wants

to better understand the creative process. See Robert Fritz, *The Path of Least Resistance: Learning to Become the Creative Force in Your Own Life.* Revised Edition. (New York: Ballantine Books, 1989).

Chapter 11: The Power of Spiritual over Material

1. Stephen R. Covey, *The Seven Habits of Highly Effective People.* (New York: Fireside, Simon and Schuster, 1990).

2. Viktor E. Frankl, *Man's Search for Meaning.* (New York: Touchstone books, 1984).

3. Ibid.

Chapter 12: Choosing Growth over Fear

1. Karen Horney, *Neurosis and Human Growth: The Struggle Toward Self-Realization.* Reissued. (New York: W. W. Norton and Company, 1991), p. 17.

2. Abraham Maslow, *The Farther Reaches of Human Nature.* (New York: Penguin Books, 1993).

3. Ibid.

Chapter 13: Stewardship: The Urge to Serve

1. Shelley E. Taylor, *The Tending Instinct: Women, Men, and the Biology of Relationships.* (New York: Times Books, Henry Holt & Co, 2003), p. 6.

2. Mohandas K. Gandhi, *Mind of Mahatma Gandhi.* Edited by R.K. Prabhu and U.R. Rao. (Ahmedabad: Navajivan Publishing, 1996).

3. Larry Dossey, *Meaning and Medicine: Lessons from a Doctor's tales of Breakthrough and Healing.* (New York: Bantam Books, 1991).

4. This study was done by David C. McClelland at Harvard University and he presented his findings in a paper titled, "Motivation and Immune Function in Health and Disease" at the meeting of the Society of Behavioral Medicine, New Orleans, March 1985. Larry Dossey cites it in his book entitled *Meaning and Medicine: Lessons from a Doctor's tales of Breakthrough and Healing.* (New York: Bantam Books, 1991), p. 176.

5. Martin Seligman, *Authentic Happiness: Using the New Positive Psychology to Realize Your Potential for Lasting Fulfillment.* (New York: Simon and Schuster Publishing, 2002).

6. Rabindranath Tagore, *Creative Unity*: (New York: The Macmillan Co, 1922).

7. Robert K. Greenleaf, *Servant Leadership: A Journey into the Nature of Legitimate Power and Greatness.* (New York: Paulist Press, 1977).

Chapter 14: Beyond Competition

1. Ashley Montagu, *Darwin: Competition and Cooperation.* (New York: Henry Schuman, 1952).

2. Alfie Kohn, *No Contest: The Case Against Competition.* (New York: Houghton Mifflin Company, 1986).

3. Phil Jackson, *Sacred Hoops: Spiritual Lessons of a Hardwood Warrior.* (New York: Hyperion, 1996).

4. Howard Schultz and Dori Jones Yang, *Pour Your Heart into it: How Starbucks Built a Company One Cup at a Time.* (New York: Hyperion, 1997).

Chapter 16: Inclusivity

Ken Wilber who is considered the "Einstein of consciousness" explains this theme of *inclusivity* very well in his book, *Boomeritis*: *A Novel that will Set You Free.* (Boston: Shambala, 2002).

Gandhi wrote this in the journal *Young India.* Mohandas K. Gandhi, *Mind of Mahatma Gandhi.* Edited by R.K. Prabhu and U.R. Rao. (Ahmedabad: Navajivan Publishing, 1996).

Chapter 17: The Power of Conscience

1. See Erich Fromm, *The Sane Society.* (New York: Owl Books, Henry Holt, 1990). Also see Erich Fromm, *Escape from Freedom.* (New York: Owl Books, Henry Holt, 1994).

Chapter 18: The Importance of Courage

1. Louis Fischer, *Mahatma Gandhi: His Life and times.* (Mumbai: Bharatiya Vidya Bhavan, 2003).

2. Martin Luther King, *Jr. A Testament of Hope: The Essential Writings and Speeches of Martin Luther King, Jr.* Edited by James M. Washington. Reprint Edition. (San Francisco: Harper San Francisco, 1991), p. 110.

Chapter 19: The Salt March and Calcutta Fast

1. These words of Nehru are cited in Joan Bondurant's book, *Conquest of Violence: The Gandhian Philosophy of Conflict.* (Berkeley: University of California Press, 1990), p. 94.

2. Jawaharlal Nehru, *Mahatma Gandhi* (Bombay: Asia Publishing House, 1965), pp. 61-63.

3. Webb Miller's report of the events at the Darsana salt works is cited in Louis Fischer's book *Mahatma Gandhi: His Life and Times.* (Mumbai: Bharatiya Vidya Bhavan, 2003), pp. 350-351.

4. E.W.R. Lumby, *The Transfer of Power in India, 1945-1947.* (London: Allen and Unwin, 1954), p. 193.

5. Judith M. Brown, *Gandhi: Prisoner of Hope.* (London: Yale University Press, 1989), p. 360.

6. Nicholas Mansergh's perceptive comments on the Calcutta Fast and its aftermath is from his book, *The Commonwealth and The Nations*, p. 142; the comments are mentioned in Dennis Dalton's book, *Mahatma Gandhi: Non-violent Power in Action* (New York: Columbia University Press, 1993, p. 159). Dalton's book provides a very detailed, well-written narration of events and analysis, of both the Salt March and the Calcutta Fast.

Chapter 20: More than Body and Mind

1. Sri Aurobindo, *A Life Divine*. (Wisconsin: Lotus Press by arrangement with Aurobindo Ashram Trust, 1990), p. 543.

2. Deepak Chopra, *Ageless Body, Timeless Mind: The Quantum Alternative to Growing Old.* (New York: Crown Publishing Group, 1994).

Chapter 21: Trust

1. R. Rosenthal and L. F. Jacobson, *Pygmalion in the Classroom* (Holt, Rinehart and Winston, 1968).

Chapter 22: The Law of Personal Responsibility

1. Mohandas K. Gandhi, *Mind of Mahatma Gandhi*. Edited by R.K. Prabhu and U.R. Rao. (Ahmedabad: Navajivan Publishing, 1996).

Chapter 23: A Sense of Mystery and Miracle

1. Carl Gustav Jung, *Memories, Dreams, Reflections*. Edited by Aniela Jaffe. Translated by Richard Winston and Clara Winston. (New York: Vintage Books, 1989), p. 354.

2. Mohandas K. Gandhi, *Mind of Mahatma Gandhi*. Edited by R.K. Prabhu and U.R. Rao. (Ahmedabad: Navajivan Publishing, 1996).

3. Abraham Maslow, *The Farther Reaches of Human Nature*. (New York: Penguin Books, 1993).

Chapter 24: The Power of Ideals

1. *The Republic of Plato*, translated by F.M. Cornford (New York: Oxford University Press, 1945), p. 176.

2. Mohandas K. Gandhi, *Mind of Mahatma Gandhi*. Edited by R.K. Prabhu and U.R. Rao. (Ahmedabad: Navajivan Publishing, 1996).

3. Ibid.

Chapter 25: Personal Honesty and Authenticity

1. See James M. Kouzes and Barry Z. Posner, *The Leadership Challenge*. 3rd Edition. (San Francisco: Jossey-Bass, 2003), p. 27.

2. Mohandas Gandhi, Gandhi: *An Autobiography, The Story of my Experiments with Truth.* Reprint Edition. (Boston, Massachusetts: Beacon Press in arrangement with Navajivan Trust, 1993).

Chapter 26: The Learning Orientation

1. Mohandas Gandhi, Gandhi: *An Autobiography, The Story of my Experiments with Truth.* Reprint Edition. (Boston, Massachusetts: Beacon Press in arrangement with Navajivan Trust, 1993).

2. Dana Sawyer, *Aldous Huxley: A Biography.* (New York: Crossroad Publishing Company, 2002), p. 143.

Chapter 27: Balancing Action and Reflection

1. Mohandas K. Gandhi, *Mind of Mahatma Gandhi.* Edited by R.K. Prabhu and U.R. Rao. (Ahmedabad: Navajivan Publishing, 1996).

Chapter 28: A Holistic Spirituality

1. Mohandas K. Gandhi, *Mind of Mahatma Gandhi.* Edited by R.K. Prabhu and U.R. Rao. (Ahmedabad: Navajivan Publishing, 1996).

2. Ibid

Chapter 29: Learning from Death

1. Mohandas K. Gandhi, *Mahatma: Life of Mohandas Karamchand Gandhi.* Edited by D.G. Tendulkar. Volume 8, 2nd Edition. (New Delhi: Publications Division, 1960), p. 205.

2. Stephen Levine, *A Year To Live: How to Live This Year As If It Were Your Last.* (New York: Three Rivers Press, 1998). Also see Elisabeth Kubler-Ross, *On Death and Dying.* Reprint Edition. (New York: Simon and Schuster, 1997).

Chapter 30: The Power of Surrender

1. Joseph Jaworski, *Synchronicity: The Inner Path to Leadership.* (San Francisco: Berrett-Koehler Publishers, 1998).

Chapter 32: The Value of Role Models and Mentors

1. Mohandas Gandhi, Gandhi: *An Autobiography, The Story of my Experiments with Truth.* Reprint Edition. (Boston, Massachusetts: Beacon Press in arrangement with Navajivan Trust, 1993).

2. Ibid.

3. Ibid.

4. Ibid.

5. Tolstoy's letter to Gandhi is cited in Louis Fischer, *Mahatma Gandhi: His Life and Times.* (Mumbai: Bharatiya Vidya Bhavan, 2003).

Chapter 34: The Power of Prioritising

1. Business Week. October 12, 2004. *The Seed of Apple's Innovation.* This article can be accessed online at www.businessweek.com.

Chapter 35: Trusteeship

1. The words in italics appear in the mission statement of the Foundation for Deep Ecology. The whole text is present on their website, www.deepecology.org.

Chapter 37; "Sarvodaya"; "For the Welfare of AH"

1. This is according to UNICEF. Please visit www.unicef.org for full details.

2. Mohandas K. Gandhi, *Mind of Mahatma Gandhi*. Edited by R.K. Prabhu and U.R. Rao. (Ahmedabad: Navajivan Publishing, 1996)

Chapter 40: Conclusion: The Hero's Journey

1. Joseph Campbell, *The Hero with a Thousand Faces*. (Princeton, New Jersey: Princeton University Press, 1990).

Bibliography and Recommended Reading

Abraham Maslow, *The Farther Reaches of Human Nature*. (New York: Penguin Books, 1993).

Abraham Maslow, *Toward a Psychology of Being*. Edited by Richard Lowry. (Hoboken, New Jersey: John Wiley, 1998).

Abraham Maslow, *Religions, Values and Peak Experiences*. (New York: Penguin Publishing, 1970).

Abraham Maslow, *Maslow on Management*. (Hoboken, New Jersey: John Wiley, 1998).

Aldous Huxley, *The Perennial Philosophy: An Interpretation of the Great Mystics, East and West*. (New York: HarperCollins, 1990).

Alfie Kohn, *No Contest: The Case Against Competition*. (New York: Houghton Mifflin Company, 1986).

Carl Rogers, *On Becoming a Person: A Therapist's View of Psychotherapy*. (New York: Houghton Mifflin Company, 1995).

Carl Jung, *Modern Man in Search of a Soul*. (Orlando: Harvest/HBJ Book, 1976).

Carl Jung, *The Portable Jung*. Edited by Joseph Campbell. Translated by R.R Hull. (New York: Penguin Publishing, 1976).

Christopher Lasch, *The Culture of Narcissism: American Life in an Age of Diminishing Expectations.* (New York: W. W. Norton & Company, 1991).

Dalai Lama and Howard Cutler, *The Art of Happiness: A Handbook for Living.* (New York: Penguin Putnam, 1998).

Dan Baker, *What Happy People Know: How the New Science of Happiness Can Change your Life for the Better.* (New York: St. Martin's Press, 2004).

Daniel Goleman, *Emotional Intelligence: Why It Can Matter More Than IQ.* (New York: Bantam Books, 1995).

David Suzuki, *The Sacred Balance: Rediscovering Our Place in. Nature.* (Vancouver. BC: GreyStone Books, 1997).

Deepak Chopra, *The Seven Spiritual Laws of Success: A Practical Guide to the Fulfillment of Your Dreams.* (San Rafael, CA: Amber Allen Publishing, 1995).

Deepak Chopra, *Ageless Body, Timeless Mind: The Quantum Alternative to Growing Old.* (New York: Crown Publishing Group, 1994).

Deepak Chopra, *How to Know God: The Soul's Journey Into the Mystery of Mysteries.* (New York: Crown Publishing Group, 2001).

Dennis Dalton, *Mahatma Gandhi: Nonviolent Power in Action.* (New York: Columbia University Press, 1993).

Eknath Easwaran, *Gandhi the Man: The Story of His Transformation.* (Tomales, CA: Nilgiri Press, 1997).

Elisabeth Kubler-Ross, *On Death and Dying.* Reprint Edition. (New York: Simon and Schuster, 1997).

Erich Fromm, *The Sane Society.* (New York: Owl Books, Henry Holt, 1990).

Erich Fromm, *Escape from Freedom.* (New York: Owl Books, Henry Holt, 1994).

Erich Fromm, *The Art of Loving.* (New York: Perennial Classics, HarperCollins, 2000).

Ernest Becker, *The Denial of Death.* (New York: Free Press, 1997).

Henry David Thoreau, *Walden and Other Writings.* (New York: Bantam Books, 1981).

Howard Schultz and Dori Jones Yang, *Pour Your Heart into it: How Starbucks Built a Company One Cup at a Time.* (New York: Hyperion, 1997).

Huston Smith, *Why Religion Matters: The Fate of the Human Spirit in an Age of Disbelief* (San Francisco: HarperCollins, 2001).

Huston Smith, *Forgotten Truth: The Common Vision of the World's Religions.* (San Francisco: HarperCollins, 1992).

Huston Smith, *The World's Religions: Our Great Wisdom Traditions.* Revised and updated edition of *The Religions of Man.* (San Francisco: HarperCollins, 1991).

Jelaluddin Rumi, *The Essential Rumi.* Translated by Coleman Barks. (San Francisco: HarperCollins, 1995).

Jiddu Krishnamurthi, *Total Freedom: The Essential Krishnamurthi*. (San Francisco: Harper Collins, 1996).

Jim Collins, *Good to Great: Why Some Companies Make the Leap... and Others Don't* (New York: HarperBusiness, 2001).

Jim Collins and Jerry Porras, *Built to Last: Successful Habits of Visionary Companies*. (New York: HarperBusiness, 2002).

Joseph Campbell, *The Hero with a Thousand Faces*. (Princeton, New Jersey: Princeton University Press, 1990).

Joseph Jaworski, *Synchronicity: The Inner Path to Leadership*. (San Francisco: Berrett-Koehler Publishers, 1998).

Irwin Yalom, *The Gift of Therapy: An Open Letter to a New Generation of Therapists and Their Patients*. (New York: HarperCollins, 2002).

Ken Wilber, *Up from Eden: A Transpersonal View of Human Evolution*. (Illinois: Quest Books, 1996).

Ken Wilber, *Grace and Grit: Spirituality and Healing in the Life and Death of Treya Killam Wilber*. (Boston: Shambala, 2001).

Ken Wilber, *No Boundaries: Eastern and Western Approaches to Personal Growth*. (Boston: Shambala, 2001).

Ken Wilber, *Boomeritis: A Novel that Will Set You Free*. (Boston: Shambala, 2002).

Ken Wilber, *Integral Psychology: Consciousness, Spirit, Psychology, Therapy.* (Boston: Shambala, 2000).

Ken Wilber, *The Essential Ken Wilber: An Introductory Reader.* (Boston: Shambala, 1998).

Lama Surya Das, *Awakening to the Sacred: Creating a Personal Spiritual Life.* (New York: Broadway Books, 2000).

Lama Surya Das, *Awakening the Buddha Within: Tibetan Wisdom for the Western World.* (New York: Broadway Books, 1998).

Lao-tzu. *The Tao Te Ching: A New English Version. Translated by Stephen Mitchell.* (New York: Harper Perennial, 1992).

Laurie Beth Jones, *The Path: Creating Your Mission Statement for Work and for Life.* (New York: Hyperion, 1996).

Louis Fischer, *Mahatma Gandhi: His Life and Times.* (Mumbai: Bharatiya Vidya Bhavan, 2003).

Martin Seligman, *Authentic Happiness: Using the New Positive Psychology to Realize Your Potential for Lasting Fulfillment.* (New York: Simon and Schuster Publishing, 2002).

Martin Luther King, *Jr. A Testament of Hope: The Essential Writings and Speeches of Martin Luther King, Jr.* Edited by James M. Washington. Reprint Edition. (San Francisco: Harper San Francisco, 1991).

Mihaly Csikszentmihalyi, *Flow: The Psychology of Optimal Experience.* (New York: Harper and Row Publishers, 1990)

Mohandas Gandhi, *Gandhi: An Autobiography, The Story of my Experiments with Truth.* (Boston, Massachusetts: Beacon Press in arrangement with Navajivan Trust, 1993).

Paramahansa Yogananda, *Autobiography of a Yogi*. (Los Angeles: Self-Realization Fellowship, 1979).

Phil Jackson, *Sacred Hoops: Spiritual Lessons of a Hardwood Warrior*. (New York: Hyperion, 1996).

Rabindranath Tagore, *Creative Unity*. (New York: The Macmillan Co, 1922).

Rainer Marie Rilke, *Letters to a Young Poet*. Translated by Stephen Mitchell. (New York: Vintage Books, 1986).

Ralph Waldo Emerson, *The Essential Writings of Ralph Waldo Emerson*. (New York: Modern Library, 2000).

Robin Sharma, *The Monk Who Sold His Ferrari: A Fable About Fulfilling Your Dreams and Reaching Your Destiny* (San Francisco: HarperCollins, 1998).

Rollo May, *Love and Will*. (New York: Dell Publishing Company, 1974).

Rollo May, *The Courage to Create*. (New York: W.W. Norton & Company, 1994).

Scott M. Peck, *The Road Less Travelled: A New Psychology of Love, Traditional Values and Spiritual Growth*. 25th Anniversary Edition. (New York: Touchstone, 2003).

Stephen Batchelor, *Buddhism Without Beliefs: A Contemporary Guide to Awakening*. (New York: Riverhead Books, 1997).

Stephen Levine, *A Year To Live: How to Live This Year As If It Were Your Last*. (New York: Three Rivers Press, 1998).

Stephen Mitchell, trans. *Bhagavad Gita: A New Translation.* (New York: Harmony Books, 2000)

Seyyed Hossein Nasr, *The Heart of Islam: Enduring Values for Humanity.* (San Francisco: HarperCollins, 2002).

Susan Taylor, *The Tending Instinct: Women, Men, and the Biology of Relationships.* (Henry Holt & Company, 2003).

Thich Nhat Hanh, *Peace is Every Step: The Path of Mindfulness in Everyday Life.* (New York: Bantam Books, 1991).

Warren Bennis, *On Becoming a Leader.* (Cambridge, Massachusetts: Perseus Publishing, 2003).

Wayne W. Dyer, *The Power of Intention: Learning to Co-create Your World Your Way.* (Carlsbad: Hay House, 2004).

William James, *The Varieties of Religious Experience.* (New York: Modern Library, 1994).

Other Resources (for personal growth and change)

www.mkgandhi.org

www.peaceisthewavgobalcommunity.org

www.robinsharma.com

www.franklincovey.com

www.drwavnedver.com

www.integralnaked.org

Resources (for those interested in volunteering)

www.volunteer.ca

www.heartandstroke.ca
The Heart and Stroke Foundation of Canada

www.dcontario.org
Distress Centres Ontario

www.davidsuzuki.org
David Suzuki Foundation

www.foecanada. org
Friends of the Earth Canada

www.sierraclub.ca
Sierra Club of Canada

www.greenpeace.ca

www.unicef.ca

www.panda.org
WWF - The Conservation Organization
